INTERPRENEUR$HIP

The Internet Entrepreneurs' Guide to

Achieving a Successful Online Business

Through Mindset, Attitude, and Evolution

Jeralyn Pasinabo Peagler

DISCLAIMER

The author has made every effort to ensure the accuracy of the information within this book was correct at time of publication. The author does not assume and hereby disclaims any liability to any party for any loss, damage, or disruption caused by errors or omissions, whether such errors or omissions result from accident, negligence, or any other cause. No part of this book is permitted for reprint without permissions from the authorized persons. For permission requests, write to the publisher, at the address below.

JP 360 Solutions, LLC

9435 Waterstone Blvd. Suite 140-2, Cincinnati, OH 45249

www.jp360solutions.com

ISBN-10: 1-7326386-0-8

ISBN-13: 978-1-7326386-0-0

InterPreneurship: The Internet Entrepreneurs' Guide to Achieving a Successful Online Business Through Mindset, Attitude, and Evolution.

TABLE OF CONTENTS

ABOUT THE AUTHOR: JERALYN PASINABO PEAGLER

Jeralyn Pasinabo Peagler is a successful interpreneur (internet entrepreneur), digital marketer, and a website blogger. She has 12 years of professional experience in the fields of business, e-commerce & operations management. She has an MBA in Ecommerce / Technology Enhanced Businesses and has been quoted in various news publications such as ABC, NBC, FOX, CBS, Digital Journal, Daily Herald, The Times and other international publications.

Jeralyn writes in-depth guides related to interpreneurship (internet entrepreneurship), e-commerce and online marketing. She is committed to promote online entrepreneurship and help internet entrepreneurs to achieve success through motivation and dedication. Jeralyn Pasinabo Peagler founded JP 360 Solutions, www.jp360solutions.com, an innovative consulting agency that provides the digital solutions for your business growth.

Before starting the JP 360 Solutions, Jeralyn Pasinabo Peagler worked 12 years in the fields of business & operation management, SEO, digital marketing, eCommerce development, online branding, technology-enhanced business & accounting.

She has developed multiple E-commerce brands making six-figure incomes in different niches. She is a certified social media marketer, SEO specialist and Google AdWords & Analytics expert.

Jeralyn Pasinabo Peagler loves learning new things every day, traveling around the world, shopping, socializing, networking while making money online.

She wants to promote interpreneurship among the younger generation and motivate them to start their own online business. Her favorite motivational quotes of all time,

"Whether you think you can or think you can't, you're right." – Henry Ford

"It is literally true that you can succeed best and quickest by helping others to succeed." - Napoleon Hill

"What you lack in talent can be made up with desire, hustle and giving 110% all the time." – Don Zimmer

You can reach Jeralyn Pasinabo Peagler at JP 360 Solutions, LLC, 9435 Waterstone Blvd. Suite 140-2, Cincinnati, OH 45249. Website: www.jp360solutions.com. Email: info@jp360solutions.com

INTRODUCTION

So, you have decided to become an interpreneur (internet entrepreneur). Maybe, you have heard of how easy it is. Now, you are determined to dive in and grab a piece of the online miracle pie for yourself. Why do you want it? It could be because you seek financial freedom, or you've discovered something amazing inside of you that you want to share with the world. It doesn't matter "why" you choose to be an online entrepreneur. The most important thing is that you are on the journey to discover massive success, it's more than you could have ever dreamed of. Over 4 billion people on the planet now have access to the internet: think about this for a moment. Your idea, no matter how silly you think it is, will fulfill someone's needs.

There are millions of internet shoppers with an open wallet ready to buy your products or services. So, why hold back? Why keep your ideas to yourself? You can gain freedom from the 9 to 5 rat race and help people with a great online business. An Interpreneur is someone whose income is mainly generated through the internet. Despite what you may have heard, there are many ways to make legit money online, all you need is the right mindset.

These days, everyone wants to be a cool entrepreneur. But, you decided to pick up this book because you know the value of learning. You have taken the first step in the right direction. You are doing what others ignore. This is why, you are the kind of person this book is written for. Someone who identifies their journey and takes the initiative to improve. This is not just a motivational or self-help book, it's for those who want to win the battle of their mind. Your mindset is where it all starts. Interpreneurship is easy only when the foundation is right.

Success or failure begins with your thoughts, your actions, and reactions. The struggle over negativity is real. People nowadays just don't understand why they can't move ahead. Without the right mindset, you will throw in the towel when times get rough. Don't get it twisted, it's easy to succeed online, but you need the right attitude and thought patterns. Your mind must align with your goals. You must believe that your business deserves to succeed like the other successful entrepreneurs.

It's easy to feel pumped up when the road is smooth. But what happens when the challenges show up? What happens when people don't buy from you? Or when you feel doubt that your business will fall into the sea of failed online ventures? Will you give up? Absolutely not!

This book will teach you how to stay motivated no matter the circumstances. You will learn how to use the power of your mind to overcome your fears and discover your untapped potentials. After reading this book, you will have no reason to keep limiting yourself. Your mindset, attitude, beliefs, thought patterns, and zeal will be transformed.

You'll realize what it takes to get started as an Interpreneur and how other successful online entrepreneurs dominate their markets. Get ready! It's time for you to break free from the mindset of lack into a reality of abundance where you are your very own superhero.

SECTION ONE:

IT ALL BEGINS IN THE MIND

CHAPTER 1

What is a Mindset?

The word "mindset" refers to the sum of your knowledge including your beliefs about the world and yourself. It represents your filter for the information you consume and put out. So, it determines how you receive and react to everything that you experience.

Mindset is often used for a specific aspect of your life, as in "the mindset of an entrepreneur" or "the growth mindset". And when it comes to achieving the things you truly want in life; the right mindset determines if you fail or succeed.

Developing the right mindset is crucial to the way you choose to learn. You have picked up this book because you are on a journey to becoming a successful online entrepreneur. Your action is not a mistake, your choice of what to read is due to your mindset. If you believe in the value of knowledge then, you'll seek out ways to gain it. Someone else who does not will most likely be watching the latest God-awful series on Netflix right now. Your mindset is made up of all the belief system you've acquired over the years. From the days of your childhood to the kind of news you consume: they all directly or indirectly influence you even if you are not aware of it.

There are good and bad types of mindsets. A good mindset will reflect your reality and help you move ahead in life. Yet, a bad mindset limits you: you become a slave of your own making.

Success in the 21st century means using what you believe in to make a positive change. You'd be surprised that by having a positive mindset, you'll make a great impact on the people who come around you. That's why your beliefs don't necessarily have to reflect your current reality. It does not mean you should be delusional but, of course the reality you believe in should be possible to an extent. That's like catch-22, but not really.

If you believe "I am a successful entrepreneur", you will act in that way. If you believe "I want to be a successful entrepreneur", you will act in this way too. The word "want" changes the impact of the sentence. It automatically signals that you are struggling for something. You'll feel more pressure than if you believe you already are. The best strategy that has worked for so many entrepreneurs worldwide is to create a belief system that seems just slightly out of reach.

The richest man in the world today, Jeff Bezos: didn't suddenly build the biggest online retail outlet ever. He started small and believed he could achieve his goals one step at a time. Amazon.com began as an idea just like you have. Jeff sold books over the internet, he believed so much in his idea that he gave up his time and money to make it a reality. At that time, selling books was not an impossible mission. As the years went by, he continually expanded his empire.

Jeff's actions show how starting from a positive place of possibilities has a huge significant impact on whether the business becomes successful or not. Believing in yourself, trusting that the product or service you're offering is valuable and having full confidence that you can overcome: is a mindset that sets the pros from the amateurs. Because it changes how you behave for the better. It lets you grow.

How to Change Your Mindset

No one is born with the right mindset. We all need to learn if we want to grow. Change is hard for many people. We clung too hard to our past belief-systems that keep us from moving forward. If you want to succeed, then you must embrace change. The world of the internet is always changing, your ability to learn what's new and quickly adapt your beliefs will make or break your business.

The following list can help you to develop the right mindset to take your business to the next level.

1. Get the Best Information

You are already off to a good start. This book is one the best investments you'll ever make on your journey to online success. Too often do young people especially fall prey to the "get rich quick" and "easy money" scams out there. The world is experiencing a high level of inequality. People are desperate for a quick fix to their money problems. Maybe, you've got student or credit card debt. These self-made gurus know that. They are exploiting your vulnerability. This is why you need to be on the lookout. The information you consume should not be opinions of amateurs. You need experts who have been there to help guide you.

Try to find the very best information in your field. Then focus on learning this information in-depth. You are not missing out on anything. Avoid the distractions that come your way and focus only on what's important.

You have to narrow down the information input to the most effective. Your ability to choose what you consume is a scarce skill that many people lack in today's click here digital age. Read great books and other information products, subscribe to some great blogs. Everything else is a waste of time.

Do all you can to avoid forums, mindless YouTube channels, and 90% of entertainment blogs. These kinds of sites encourage procrastination and information overload. Only a tiny fraction of the information out there is really worth the read. You have to develop the skill of identifying this kind of information. We are talking about the right mindset here; part of it is not to get sucked into the mediocre area. You want to align yourself with the best available options.

2. Role Model the Best People

Similar to the first point, search for the top masters in your field. Study what they do (not just what they say) and model their actions. Adopt their kind of thinking and mindset. Follow them on social media. Of course, only use what applies to you and your business. That way you can actually improve and personalize their mindset to fit perfectly for you. It's not copying, it's taking what works for you by getting inspiration and quality input.

Your best bet is to do a Google search for outstanding people in your niche. Don't just follow them on Twitter. Read their biographies, you'd be surprised how inspiring they can be.

Seth Gordin, a founder of Squidoo and a former dot.com executive is a great example to start with. He knows a lot about the ups and downs of running an online business. In 2014, he had to give his most successful company to the competition because of Google. Squidoo was the best revenue sharing article writing site ever created. A lot of people made a living writing for the site. Unfortunately, the bad apples infiltered the site. Google's analytics was unhappy with that and the site was blacklisted, leading to a sharp decline in page views. It was a sad day for the internet when Squidoo died because none of the alternatives even came close. Seth continues to publish widely successful books, but he has not been involved in any major dot.com business. You can learn from his massive failure and subsequent success.

It's important that you learn about the people who failed and not just the winners. This gives a much better perspective of what it takes to achieve success.

3. Examine Your Current Beliefs

What is your current belief-systems? Are these beliefs supporting your ambitions? Or are there self-limiting beliefs? You have to identify those possible blocks and turn them around. Because whether you know about limiting beliefs or not, they influence you through your subconscious mind.

To uncover your beliefs, take some time to ask yourself the right questions about where you want to go and what is standing in your way right now. You can turn those beliefs around by continually declaring the positive versions. You can make use of affirmations to help you quickly overcome your old limiting mindsets. Remember to keep at it until you notice a real change in not just what goes on your mind: but, also your behavior.

4. Shape Your Mindset with Vision and Goals

The most effective way to quickly change your mindset is to change your goals. Seeing the images in your mind's eye that describes your end result creates a strong pull towards your goals.

Be always willing to learn and adapt from your own experience. Also, try to look deeper for the real reasons why you are not getting the results you desire. When you achieve any of your set goals, make sure you write down what motivated you to do it. Doing this will create an experienced tracker that will help keep you on the trail for continuous success.

5. Find Your Voice

In the world of internet marketing, your voice is your brand. It's what makes you stand out among the millions of others doing the same thing you're doing. Without a strong voice, your brand can't penetrate the market. People need to resonate with your brand story. You can achieve that through a powerful voice that speaks your truth. Depending on what niche you're in, you can either use a personal or professional voice. A personal voice is best for health, fitness, fashion, gardening, and beauty niches. Generally, any business that caters to a very intimate aspect of people's life should have a personal voice. The professional voice is used in niches where people respect authority more and buy big businesses. A dentist promoting his practice, an affiliate marketer, and real estate agents are all examples of businesses that need to use a professional tone.

To help you find your voice, answer these questions to clear your mind:

- What are you most skilled at?

- What do you love doing?

- What niche are you serving?

- Who's your target audience?

- Where do you have the most experience?

- Are you an expert? Whether your expertise is required depends on your chosen niche.

- And finally, what is life asking of you? What gives your life meaning and purpose? What do you feel like you should be doing? In short, what is your conscience directing you to do?

Your voice is what you express 100% authentically, it is the unique thing that you can add to the world, because you are who you are. Your voice won't just affect your customers, it will reshape your mindset too. As you begin to use the words that suit you, your mind adapts. Stay open and flexible in your mind. But, don't be too flexible. It's important that you come to terms with your voice because what we say and how we say it: are powerful tools that silently define our reality.

6. Protect Your Mindset

No matter what you do or what you don't do, people will judge you. We are constantly attacked for what we believe in. There will be naysayers who will try their best to pull you down. This is why it's important that you protect your mindset. You don't have to tell everyone the details of your life and business. Avoid telling people your goals. If you must then, reveal it to only those who are closest to you. When you open yourself too much to others, you become an easy target for negativity. People who have no idea about your vision will suddenly want to give you business advice. It's best to keep your mindset hidden if you don't want to face constant debate in your mind about what steps to take next. Because the advice you receive won't fall on deaf ears, you mind consumes it. And this will have an impact on your decision-making process.

CHAPTER 2

What is Positive Thinking?

Positive thinking has become a popular mantra in modern society. Some people think it's supposed to magically solve all their problems. But that's far from what it is. People who say, "With positive thinking, you can do just about anything", are either ignorant or living in Utopia.

Negative thinking is bad for you both physically and mentally. Still, that does not mean once you start thinking positive you don't need to do any actual work. What positive thinking does is help you use your ability to succeed faster. Yeah, there are many negative people who've become a millionaire and even billionaires: they are unhappy. Most of them are probably on antidepressant drugs because of all the hate they keep inside. You can avoid this with positive thinking. We have always been taught that success comes with a price, that's true. Positive thinking creates the mindset that makes you overcome the adversities that you will stumble upon on your journey to success.

Negativity is toxic: it poisons the mind. You can't see clearly; your emotions go out of control because negativity breeds fear.

You choose between positive thinking and negative thinking: the difference is that with positive thinking your outcome will not be determined in either disappointment, feeling like a failure or even depression.

So, if you choose to have positive mindset, you make the best choice. It will change your self-image, will get you the best results and will allow you to meet amazing people who support your dream.

What Exactly is Positive Thinking?

"The mental attitude which leads to expectations of favorable and good outcomes is known as positive thinking."

As kids, we experienced with negativity more than positive situations. By the time a child is 18 years old, he or she's been told 'no' or 'you can't do it' an estimated 148,000 times.

Irrespective of the culture you grew up in, this seems to be the reality most of us had.

Negativity is built into human nature, positivity is the exception. No one teaches a child how to lie, hit, or take what's not theirs. People naturally think negative. So, you're not alone in this. The media are not helping to make the situation better. Although terrorism and poverty rates has declined, the media still repeats past images to keep us in a state of fear. The sad reality is that the media influences us much more than we like to admit.

Our environment makes it easy to be pessimistic. You must not give into it. Your growth and success depend on what you see in your mind. You need to admit words, thoughts, and images that support your goals. The last thing you want is to stand in the way of your progress. Your terminology, the way you use language that shows yourself and others how you think.

You might know a lot of negative thinking people around you. From the person that keeps complaining about what's wrong, and that everything is going to turn out for the worst (even the weather) to the unaware negative thinker: you encounter these people daily. It's unavoidable, But, you can decide to be pessimistic.

Where's Your Focus?

There is a universal truth that even the cavemen can relate to. And, that is, whatever you focus on expands. Attention is a very valuable currency. As an entrepreneur, you need to be in charge of who and what gets your attention. You can do a mind exercise with a friend to see for yourself that our mind filters only what we find important enough to remember or whatever kind of assignment we give it.

It is impossible to run a business and not have to deal with the hiccups that come along with it. If you focus on the struggles, your mind goes into a defeated mode. You automatically sabotage your efforts.

Negative thinking does not see what's already there. You'll ignore the everyday small success that ultimately leads to you achieving your big goals. You will find it difficult to start and accomplish any objectives or tasks.

To have a positive mindset means to focus on what is there, instead, of focusing on what isn't there.

Take a moment to appreciate what you have right now –
you most likely have a place you can call 'home', some money
in the bank and access to the internet.

Yes, you do have something in your life to be grateful for.
Many dream of starting a business but never acted on it. You
have gone farther than most people will ever reach. Your
business goals may still seem far from your reach, but,
focusing your mind on what's not going right won't help you.

This is not saying you should ignore negative feedback or
mistakes, you need to evaluate your failures. As the saying
goes, "let failure go to your head and success go to your
heart". A positive mindset is not a hippie mindset. It means
you acknowledge the negativity while focusing on what
you're doing right.

When you give your attention to positive thinking, you
stay motivated to start and finish that project.

How Do You See the World?

Witness bias is when different people experience the same
event but give varied accounts of what happened. This is very

common because the human memory is flawed. Our experience of reality depends on our perception.

For example, two children with their parents at an amusement park; one of them enjoys the Mary-go-round ride, but the other cries loudly. It's the same ride, just different perceptions. One experiences fun while the other feels fear.

Our brain receives more than four billion bits of information every second and it needs to decide or select what is most important and what is not. Through this process, we create our unique map of the world. It filters what we see, feel, hear and taste.

The best strategy for changing your negative perceptions is taking note of them and consciously reminding yourself of the positive truths.

When you focus on your thoughts consciously, you take control of your thoughts and you can redirect them towards a more positive mindset. By focusing on what's good in your life, and not what's missing or what doesn't work, you change your point of view and thus your results.

Seeing the Opportunity

To think positively means seeing possibilities in what others consider as a problem. Negative thinking stalls your innovative abilities. You'll find it difficult to recognize opportunities. Building a successful online business requires you to quickly see trends. Whether it's Search Engine Marketing or hashtag on Twitter, when a new trend begins which favors your brand: you want to recognize it as soon as possible. This gets people's attention and will get your brand noticed.

Sometimes, the whole picture may not be complete, some of the pieces of the puzzle may be missing, but once you see the big picture in your mind: you must act on it. This will help you realize your goals despite all visible limitations. Thinking positively is not all about seeing the good side only and ignoring the effects and dangers that come along with the goodies of life.

It goes beyond overlooking the challenges that are standing before you and ignoring the roadblocks ahead of you. Positive thinking means walking the road with a clear picture of your destination in your mind. This keeps you excited as you move on. It gives you the strength and courage to find a way out of every huddle and gets you motivated to keep on going.

Self-esteem

Your level of self-esteem is the fundamental factor that determines whether you are successful or not. The more value you place on yourself, the more successful you will become as this create self-motivation. Your success becomes a product of your effort. When you know that you are making progress and getting results, you will be motivated to find ways of improving by increasing your effort and being more efficient.

Do what makes you feel good and positive towards yourself and your life, it will help to build up your self-esteem and improves your level of mental fitness. Achieving one of your goals strengthens your self-esteem and builds your self-confidence.

"Success is the foundation for greater success." This is a simple truth many entrepreneurs ignore. Putting more effort and surviving the storm in your business helps you grow. You won't just get more customers or make more money: you'll be happier because your self-worth increases.

The way you see yourself determines your thought patterns. However, thinking positively will not be of any good to an individual who sees his/herself as a failure. This is why it is important that you change the way you see yourself from a negative perspective into a positive light.

Having a negative view about one's self-creates a lack of willingness to stop self-destructive habits such as hanging out with the wrong kind of people.

It's normal to feel unworthy, and the fear that the market will not accept you. It's tempting to be fake these days online. But, don't give in. Stay true to yourself.

However, if you are in high school, you will know that at this stage of life, most people do not have a vivid mental picture of who they are and this makes them divide classes into two groups: the active ones and the passive ones.

If you feel positive about yourself, you wouldn't care what other people think about you. All you need to do is improve on your self-image.

Young people are more likely to easily lose their focus, and this could be caused by a lot of external influences. The most common one being our constant exposure to digital and electronic devices. Video games and the internet affects the self-esteem of many in our digital age. Cyberbullying is a problem and so is video game addiction. Being judged by hateful strangers on the internet impacts our self-perception. Video games, on the other hand, makes it difficult for you to socialize and live in the real world.

Don't borrow your ideas of yourself from people who have no idea who they are themselves. Believe in your hustle, focus on you and practice positive self-talk daily.

How to Start Thinking Positive

Most people say "think positive" when their friend, family-member, spouse or acquaintance is feeling a bit down or has to deal with a certain problem. But hardly anybody takes these powerful words seriously.

Despite the high popularity of positive thinking, the majority of us don't actually implements them. The reality is that it's easier to say think positive than doing it.

Thinking positively means changing your mental, emotional, psychological and your physical state: towards yourself, others and situations.

Affirmations is the most powerful tool to put your mind in a focused state. Another medium is listening to motivational speeches daily. You can find these on YouTube.

You would agree that words, such as 'optimistic', 'success', 'rich', luck' and 'happy' convey stronger positive imagery in your mind than words such as 'okay', 'reasonable', 'guess', even 'depressed'.

Constantly hearing and speaking positive words reshape your mindset faster than you can imagine. Evan Carmichael, a YouTube and internet entrepreneur uses daily motivation to keep him focused. Achieving success is no sprint, it's a marathon. Along the way, you'll get bruised and suffer defeat: thinking positive is your best armor in times when you'll feel like giving it all up.

They say motivation does not last but neither does taking a bath. You need an audio or video affirmations and motivational talks from gurus to keep that fire burning inside of you.

Now positive thinking on its own is not enough to create long lasting results in life. But, it's true that you become what you constantly think about. Your thoughts are a result of your beliefs, which then determine your personality, attitude, behavior and ultimately your results.

It's what you tell yourself in words, pictures and thoughts that your mind will translate into reality. Since your mind is built to serve you in the best way possible, it will conduct everything necessary to match the thoughts you have about yourself, your life and your results.

It's therefore absolutely necessary to have a positive mindset and to tell yourself positively, empowering and supporting messages daily. Think about this quote by Ralph Waldo Emerson, "Sow a thought, and you reap an act. Sow an act, and you reap a habit. Sow a habit and you reap a character. Sow a character and you reap a destiny".

Everything that we use today including smartphones and the internet was once a figment of someone's imagination. Disregard negative thoughts. Refuse to think such thoughts and replace them with constructive happy thoughts. Stop limiting yourself, you are capable of doing so much more. But, first, you must see this reality in your mind's eye.

CHAPTER 3

Positive Attitude

People will describe you by the way you present yourself and how you react to situations. Face it, bad things happen in life. Sometimes, you give it your all and things just don't go your way. You're having a great day, then suddenly one crappy phone call ruins it. You may not have control of everything that happens to you, but you decide how you'll react to it.

Positive attitude differs from positive thinking, it refers to how you respond towards people and events. Most of us will immediately react badly when we encounter negativity, it's natural.

If you're always grumpy and talking yourself down, most likely people are going to perceive you as a negative person. If you choose to be cheerful and approach life with a positive attitude, people are more likely to view you as someone who is fun to be around.

Developing a positive attitude leads to opportunities for growth in your life and business. Every company has those customers that no matter what you do, they'll never be satisfied. It's not about what people do to you, but how you respond. It's much harder to transform your attitude than your thinking process. Still, if you decide to make a lasting change and stick to it, you'll eventually affect your subconscious mind positively.

Your attitude is described as a settled way of thinking or feeling about someone or something, typically one that is reflected in your behavior. It can be either positive or negative. A positive attitude shows that you are functioning within an optimistic state of mind. Combined with positive thinking, and optimism, a positive attitude is the root of lasting success. Studies show that positive people are more successful and cope better with stress because they understand that positivity is more than just an attitude, it's a lifestyle.

Overall, people with a positive attitude believe that good things will come their way because they can control their reactions to what life throws at them.

When something bad happens, a person with a positive attitude chooses to look at the incident as isolated and beyond their control while consistently searching for ways to make the best of the situation: remaining positive towards the future. Most people do the complete opposite. Don't assumed that every bad thing that happened was because bad things always seemed to happen to you and would continue to always happen. Instead, look for ways to make the best of the situation. Being angry and frustrated only increases your stress levels.

What's important to understand though, is that attitudes are habits that you can change. Creating and applying a positive attitude to everyday life takes practice.

Your thoughts are always under your control. Deciding to give your energy and attention to positivity opens shut doors and creates amazing relationships. Negative customers will be converted to people who leave good feedback. Because the internet is filled with so much hate, your online business will thrive as we are attracted to people with a positive attitude.

Some powerful ways to develop a positive attitude are:

1. Practice having a positive outlook on life. Take some time to look at your life, the plans you have for yourself, and the way you deal with people and situations on a day-to-day basis. Do you always focus on the negative aspects of every situation or are you actively looking for ways to improve them? Do you view your life as pointless because you can't seem to get anywhere or do you refuse to give up and constantly strive to reach your goals? If you're going to have a positive outlook, you need a positive attitude and vice versa.

2. Consider what you would like to happen in your health, relationships and business. Develop a plan that gives you a sense of direction and a feeling of purpose. Look for steps you can take to make your goals more attainable. Always believe that you are capable of reaching your goals because you are.

3. Keeping a positive attitude helps you set positive goals and develop your self-confidence. Trust yourself and visualize your ambitions. Create an action plan and take the initiative to pursue it. Don't dwell on what you

haven't accomplished yet. Rather, focus on what you have and remind yourself of all of the great accomplishments you'll make in the future.

4. Encourage others. Showing appreciation, courtesy and encouragement towards others is a great way to develop a positive attitude and enhance your positive thinking. Say 'thank you', smile often, show positivity and sincerity in everything you do. Don't get discouraged because something great happened for someone else before it happened for you. Congratulate them on their success and believe that your hard work is going to pay off. Everyone appreciates the person who stays positive and encouraging through their own success and the success of others.

CHAPTER 4

Thinking Patterns and Your Mindset

Ever wondered what it is that separates the go-getters from the people who sit on their a** just waiting for the perfect situations? The go-getters are proactive people while the waiters are reactive people.

Proactive people believe that success is of their own making; it's their responsibility to make things happen. They also believe that they have the skills and ability to make things happen and get things done. Reactive people wait for situations to present themselves before addressing them. Reactive people tend to have low self-confidence than proactive people.

If you're going to embrace a positive mindset, then you must start challenging yourself to take initiative and make things happen. You can't be afraid to fail. Have faith in yourself and your abilities. Ask yourself if you want to be the person who is making things happen and going places, or would you rather spin your wheels waiting for opportunities to present themselves.

How to Start Taking the Initiative

1. First things first; proactive people start their day with a positive attitude. Proactive people speak and act with confidence. Self-confidence is extremely important for living a positive life. Self- confidence is readily achievable; all you need is the determination to achieve it. When developing self-confidence the first thing you should do is reflect on the things you've already achieved. Look back on the things you've done in life that you are most proud of. And reflect on the success you've already had. Next, take the time to reflect on your strengths, weaknesses, opportunities and threats (SWOT). Use the SWOT analysis to assess what you're good at (strengths), where you could improve (weaknesses), what opportunities are available for you to take initiative (opportunities): use your strengths and consider what types of obstacles you are facing (threats).

Once you've analyzed your strengths and weaknesses, eliminate negative self-talk from your vocabulary. Proactive people practice building their self-confidence by consistently telling themselves "I can" and "I will". This is called thought awareness. You make the choice to fill your mind with encouraging words.

Take the initiative to develop a positive mindset and you will activate the proactive individual inside just waiting to get out.

2. Challenge your way of doing things. Remember, a positive attitude is more than just a mindset; it's a way of living. This is a habit you have to develop. Some of the best initiatives you can take are making small changes to old routines. Look for ways to be more efficient, make what you're doing a little more enjoyable and get acquainted with taking small risks that is worth your time.

3. Always look for opportunities. If you want to be a go-getter, you have to stay on your toes. Practice looking at what you're doing, what others are doing, and what can be done for improvement. Positive people are

constantly looking for ways to grow. The trick is to train your mind to be observant and do this consistently.

Learning to take initiative helps you practice positivity. It takes self-confidence to be a proactive person and it often takes practice to develop this kind of thinking. You have what it takes to discover and create the opportunities and success you desire.

Accurate Thinking

Accurate thinking involves thinking with our minds and not our emotions. Practicing a positive attitude requires learning to evaluate and react to events without allowing your emotions get in the way. Making decisions based on emotions has the potential to cause judgmental behavior and decision making errors: which creates negative thought patterns.

Accurate thinking places the situation you are facing into proper perspective, while, positive thinking replaces any negative thoughts with positive and structured thoughts.

In order to develop accurate thinking (which will help influence our positive thinking), we need to first understand that we are in control of what we think. When we use our minds to control our emotions we are then able to control our actions. When we are in control of our thinking, we are in control of our lives. This is of significant importance.

Secondly, practicing accurate thinking involves learning that we are in control of our outlook on life. Our outlook on life is influenced by the events that induce our thinking; our basic life outlook is based on past experiences. What we must understand is that, our outlook on life is generally developed at a young age when we are most susceptible to influence.

For example, you may have been bullied at school and now you resent authority. You feel anyone who has an advantage over you is a threat to your wellbeing. What you should realized though, is that you now have the ability to change that outlook.

This isn't going to be easy but it's not impossible to do either. Changing our outlook is achieved by training ourselves to focus on the positive rather than the negative. Developing a positive attitude lifts you up, while dwelling in a negative attitude is like pressing your self-destruct button over and over again.

Our attitude determines the person we are and the way others see us. Our attitude is a reflection of our thinking and our emotions. When you are thinking accurately and positively, as we all should be, other people are going to see you as an upbeat and happy person who's in control of their life. Once you have gained control of your thoughts (positive thinking) and emotions (accurate thinking), your attitude will automatically follow the path you are paving with positivity.

Accurate thinking is an incredibly powerful tool that enables us to strengthen our positive thinking and control our thoughts, emotions, and actions no matter the situation. This removes the emotion from important decision making every time. We cannot control the actions, thoughts or words of others. All we can do is control how we conduct ourselves in response to other individuals and different situations as life presents them.

Choosing to respond positively through accurate thinking is one of the best decisions you will ever make.

Enthusiasm

Enthusiasm is optimism on steroids: it's a big part of having a positive attitude and staying motivated. In fact, enthusiasm and a positive attitude is what you need to push you through the tough times. Enthusiasm is infectious: passionate people are amazing, but enthusiast stands out amongst the crowds. This pulls people to your brand, let's face it who doesn't love the guy who is always upbeat and sees possibilities.

No one is born an enthusiast, it's a learned skill. To help your business thrive online, here are 10 strategies for developing and practicing enthusiasm:

1. Start with passion. You need to be excited about what you are doing if you are going to outwardly portray enthusiasm. Passion and positivity are what keep your enthusiasm high even when things get a little rough. Basically, if you love what you do, enthusiasm won't be much of a problem.

2. Show gratitude. One of the best ways to build up your enthusiasm is to remind yourself of what you have, what you've accomplished, and to be thankful for it. It's so easy to get sidetracked and forget about the little things that make our lives enjoyable. Take the time to be thankful for who you are and for every experience that got you here.

3. Stay positive. Enthusiasm can't thrive in a negative environment. If you can teach yourself to dwell in a positive attitude, enthusiasm will skyrocket you towards your goals by helping you practice positive actions.

4. Take pride in what you do. Be enthusiastic about your brand and take pride in it. Talk about what you're proud of and why you're proud of it. Taking pride in your well-earned accomplishments is positive reinforcement for your self-confidence.

5. Be creative. You can never be too creative. Creativity builds enthusiasm and enthusiasm builds creativity. If you want a fast and effective way to boost either of these, practice, practice and practice.

6. Strive to be the initiator. Being proactive will get you noticed. People who are proactive show a sense of enthusiasm unmatched by people who are reactive.

7. Be understanding and reasonable. Enthusiasm won't grow in an unreasonable or unrealistic environment. Keep a little flexibility, stay willing to compromise and

listen to others. Enthusiasm grows with teamwork alongside a sense of contribution and belonging.

8. Learn to be patient. You want enthusiasm that will last forever. If your enthusiasm goes on and off, you're not sincere in your efforts and you need to reassess what you're doing and why you're doing it.

9. Realize you don't have to be agitated, stressed or be under the influence of drugs to portray enthusiasm. Enthusiasm can be experienced in stillness and contentment with what you have achieved and what you hope to achieve.

10. Evolve. When you understand that you are taking steps to get better at what you do every day, always looking for ways to grow and improve: it's hard not to get excited. Be aware of the purpose and meaning of everything you do. When you're enthusiastic about your brand and your business strategies, the only thing that can stop you is yourself.

Enthusiasm and a positive mindset go hand in hand. You can't have one without the other. Dive into your business, master it and enjoy every step of the way.

Self-doubt

In our modern society of social media and shallow reactions, most people can't help doubting themselves. One swipe on Facebook or Instagram shows a friend that's doing much better than you. You still feel this way even when your mind tells you they are faking it.

The feelings of fear, rejection, inferiority, inadequacy, and guilt are all products of thought patterns we believe about ourselves from childhood.

It's not that successful people don't suffer from this kind of emotions, they just learn to master and deal with their emotions better. Majority of people have failed to recognize this secret and that is why they have not been successful. So, you must discover and use your ability to overcome self-doubt: speak to yourself, say positive and self-motivating words. On your journey to success, you will have to face thoughts of self-doubt. When this happens, write out your negative thoughts and calmly tell yourself how you will overcome negativity with positivity and enjoy the fruits of your success.

Open your mind to learn new things. Be aware of your inner voice. Constantly remind yourself that your journey is personal, life is not a competition. Take a bold step at a time and keep your eyes on the price.

Resonance

When you think positively on a daily basis, it's like tuning a piano to get the right C-note; you need to adjust the string one at a time. So, when you are in tune, everything around you on the same level will produce the right sounds.

The same happens when people who are like-minded, goal oriented, success-focused and positive thinkers associate. Being success-focused means that you have a positive mindset. Have you ever heard of a successful person always saying, "I don't think this will work for me", or "why is this happening to me all the time?"

Successful and unsuccessful people are different in just a few minor things and this is basically on their thinking patterns. Warren Buffett, one of most successful investors of all time, always advice people to watch their circle of friends.

Do you know Bill Gates and Warren Buffett have been friends for more than 27 years? One is a tech entrepreneur, and the other is an investor: still, their minds are operating on a similar frequency.

Successful people remain goal oriented, focused, determined and positive. This does not mean that they are not sometimes faced with failures and challenges, but they are determined to overcome it. They never give up until they have achieved their goal. Make sure the people in your circle reflect your goals. Invest in meaningful friendships: avoid the naysayers, even if they are family.

What separates those who achieve success from the others who fail is their thought pattern. You can't have a downward thinking process and expect success. No, your mind must align with your direction. It's not an impossible mission to reshape your thought patterns. But, you must commit and continually practice daily if you truly desire long-lasting change.

SECTION TWO:

THE ONLINE MARKETER'S MINDSET

REVOLUTION

CHAPTER 5

Creative Vision

Creativity isn't a skill reserved for writers and artists. Creativity is about developing new ways for solving problems and approaching situations. This is especially useful when it comes to fostering a positive attitude. When life throws you a box of coal, you need creativity to turn the situation around. Without your imagination, you'll be stuck in a harsh reality.

You don't need to be a genius to use your creative mind. We all have imaginations. Most of us lose the ability to properly use the mind's eye as we grew up. We were told to pay attention and avoid daydreaming. Well, sometimes, seeing can be deceiving.

Some tips to help you boost your positive thinking creativity are:

- Commit to developing your creative skills. Don't put this off. Take some time each day and put effort to think of new and useful ways you can create opportunities and approach stressful situations.

- Reward your curiosity. Give yourself the chance to explore new topics and approaches. Compense yourself for taking the initiative to think outside the box and try something new.

- Take risks. When it comes to developing your creative vision, the point is to take risks and try out untested waters. You may not always succeed but you are going to boost your creativity in the process: creating more opportunities to implement your positive and accurate thinking. If things don't go according to plan, congratulate yourself on discovering what won't work and keep looking for what will.

- Face your fear of failure. Don't let mistakes paralyze your progress. Remind yourself that every business goes through phases of ups and downs: mistakes are part of progress. Through your positivity and creativity you will reach your goals.

- Keep track of your progress and review it often. Intentionally build your self-confidence by reflecting on and taking pride in the things you've accomplished. Commend your efforts and stay on the lookout for even more ways to be creative.

- Make time to develop your creativity. Practice, practice, practice. You can't overdo this. Practice is what separates masters from amateurs.

- Realize that most problems have multiple solutions. Take the time to consider them all. Use accurate thinking to explore the possibilities.

- Create opportunities for creativity by taking initiative and volunteering for new projects or develop new tools for current projects.

You develop creative vision through fearless use of your imagination. It takes guts to let your imagination run wild and go with your instincts; it takes a lot of self-confidence too.

If you believe in yourself and remain positive while searching for new ways to do things, there's no way you can fail. Because giving up is the true definition of failure.

Don't misunderstand me, you may not always reach the goal you want to achieve on the first try. Even if you try and fail, never give up. Learn new skills and strategies for overcoming obstacles.

Jack Ma, the founder, and CEO of Alibaba group failed at almost everything he did before his massive success with online retail. He learned, experimented and continued to forge ahead in spite of fears. His success today is directly correlated to the lessons he learned and applied from his past failures.

Creative vision and operating with a positive attitude involves taking everything you've learned, whether by failure or success and implementing it into your strategy for your future endeavors.

CHAPTER 6

Breaking the Mental Barriers

These days everyone is an instant internet millionaire. Self-proclaimed gurus on YouTube rent flashy cars, houses among other things to deceive gullible minds. Why would anyone who makes $10 million a year need you to buy their $29.99 course? The sad truth is there are more scammers than real stories. Building a successful online business goes beyond creating a website or finding a product. Just as in an offline business, your mind, and body need to align on your pursuit of success. There are always barriers to achieving anything worthwhile in life. The journey to achieving your goals is not supposed to be easy, so don't expect it to be. However, if you prepare your mind ahead, you'll have a better chance of overcoming the obstacles than others.

Believe

Everything in life starts with a belief. It is important that you believe your goals are attainable: if you don't have a belief to succeed, you won't.

- Be positive

- Learn from your past mistakes

- Learn to forgive yourself and don't let past failures affect your future success

- Avoid any negative thought process

- Stick to a proven plan

- Enjoy – love – life – vitality

Understanding the Why Principle

"There are two great days in a person's life - the day we are born and the day we discover why". - **William Barclay**

Have you heard of Napster? I'm betting your answer is No. Napster was a free peer-to-peer music sharing website created by two young American boys back in 1999: It was the first of its kind. The site became so popular it almost destroyed the music industry. The creators of the site, Sean Parker, and Sean Fanning had to shut it down in 2001 because of copyrights issues.

Now, why is this important? These two 19 years old programmers loved listening to music, but hated going to the store to buy it. They discovered that it was easier to listen to music on their computer, and they could even share it online. This simple thought became the reason for their hard work to build the site.

They used the power of the "why principle" to invent the online media streaming industry we know and love today. It was not easy for them, they had to face the big record labels and their army of lawyers: but they kept insisting that streaming is the next big step that the music industry needs to grow.

When you know why you do the things you do, the challenges will not make you give up. So many people make plans but never actually do any of them.

If you knew that your life depended on waking up by 5:00 am every morning, I bet you would not hesitate to make it a reality. This is the success mindset you need. Even though the original Napster is no more, the creators are now billionaires. But, even better is we now enjoy the gift of their persistence.

Before getting started on any project, take a moment to ask yourself why is this important to me and is this the one thing that will move me towards achieving my goals? It does not matter if you are starting a freelance business, YouTube vlog or an App: you need to understand why. Knowing the reason why you have that goal will help your brain release a boost of energy to keep you going no matter what.

Progress is what defines us as human beings. It makes us happy: It improves our self-worth and self-confidence. Why should people buy from you?

Understanding why you deserve to attain your set goals makes the difference between dreamers and achievers. The future generations depend on us to leave a better than average legacy. Through the power of your mind, you can reshape your life towards a place of happiness and fulfillment. So be brave, pick up a pen and write down your ultimate goals for your business. Put the notes somewhere you can always see them so that you are constantly reminded of your why. Doing this supercharges your mind to stay focused and keep going.

SECTION THREE:

BUILDING AN ONLINE BUSINESS

FROM SCRATCH

CHAPTER 7

The Limitless Opportunity

Do you know of a better time in human history when single motivated individuals can accumulate so much wealth than today? The simple answer is none. Jeff Bezos has more money than the top 400 richest people published by Forbes in 1982.

What does this mean for you? Forget about the horrible media, they are there to sell fear. The economy is bad, yet over 1,000 people become new millionaires every day. You know what's causing this? It's the internet. You can literally reach over 5 billion people through your online business. Oil and gas are no longer the most valuable commodity: online data is. You too can take a slice of the pie. Don't believe that there's too much competition out there. The market is overflowing with potential customers. All you need to do is meet the overwhelming demand with supply. Give the market what it wants.

How to Make the Most Impact with Your Online Business

Find Your Niche

- Find a popular niche that you know something about, or a niche you are willing to invest time learning about. Don't forget if you know more about a subject than your prospect, you become the go-to person everyone listens to for expert advice.

- Write a free report, short eBook or other types of lead magnets on your chosen subject. Then, use this offer to build your mailing list. As long as what you're offering is valuable, people will show up. This does not apply if you are an information entrepreneur. You may need to find a balance between what information you give free and the ones you're selling: or else, no one will buy from you.

- Distribute free information on a popular blog or social media. Remember to invite people to subscribe to your mailing list. Soon, your email addresses will grow and you will have a list to promote and sell relevant products. Doing this will build your credibility and people will trust you in the future.

- You should be...

     i. S – Specific

     ii. M –Measurable

     iii. A - Achievable

     iv. R - Realistic

     v. T - Timed

Using SMART as a way to assess your goals makes it easier to achieve them.

Most people lack confidence and have little faith in their own abilities. This mentality is only a belief which should be discarded. There must be something you are good at. The way you think will ultimately affect what you achieve in life: if you expect nothing then you will get nothing. Thinking positive and concentrating on your strengths gives you the mental stamina you need to keep going.

The Market Always Comes First

In order for any product to be successful, it must have a mass audience. It's no use creating a product or offering a service that very few people will be interested in. You can do it, but, it's much difficult to find success this way.

Before deciding on your products niche, you must first do some market research. And, study your competition to see if you can improve on what is already on offer. We are not trying to re-invent the wheel here, make sure that can exceed people's expectations. Or else, you become just another seller.

The basic steps to creating a successful online business in simple terms are...

1. Find a popular market that has thousands of hungry to buy prospects

2. Give that market exactly what it wants

3. Rinse and repeat

Some of the most Profitable niches on the internet are...

1. Work from home, i.e., eBay, clickbank, internet marketing, MLM etc.

2. Health and fitness, i.e., dieting, exercise, body building etc.

3. How to manuals in every popular topic, i.e., computer skills, getting a better job, education, investment, gambling, etc.

You don't have to create products in these niches. If you've done your research and it confirms the demand, then go ahead and implement your ideas.

Develop Your Idea

Inspiration is free; however, the very best ideas still need developing. A good starting point is to write down your ideas, then go through the list to make sure that:

1. You're knowledgeable on the subject;

2. You're reaching the biggest market audience;

3. People are willing to buy.

Yes, there are some products or services that people are not willing to buy online. An affiliate website on expert services is not always the best idea. A medical or other expert field requires some credibility. Unless you can prove that your business addresses the customers worries, you should avoid any niche of concern.

The best way to develop your ideas is to break them down into smaller parts. Begin from the task that is most feasible to the more difficult ones.

Outline Your Business Plan

When you fail to plan, you plan to fail. Business plans are so crucial to your success that ignoring it can ruin your weeks or even months of hard work. You don't need to be too strict with your plans, but it should at least be clear what your long-term strategy is.

Prepare for Marketing

Properly marketing your product is paramount to its success. You must be professional in your approach, which means you need great presentation. Your business should be presented in a way your target audience will understand. There are various means of promoting your online venture: some are paid while others are not.

Online Marketing Strategies

Every day hundreds and thousands of ideas are created & millions of business initiatives are created but still only very few of them succeeds. Only a few attract the customers and become big brands like Alibaba, Amazon, Tesla or SpaceX. That's where the marketing strategy counts.

Marketing is all about showing the right product to the right people at the right moment. Internet marketing is different from traditional marketing. You can just put a road sign and wait for your customers to see and check into your shop. So, what does it take to market your business online?

Search Engine Optimization (SEO)

The first step is less costly but takes some time. It's called Search Engine Optimization (SEO). SEO is great for long term results. You will prepare your website to rank high on the search engine and people will begin to see your website at the Search Engine Result Pages (SERP). More visibility means more traffic and more traffic means more sales opportunity.

But it certainly takes time. The process also needs lots of technical knowledge and resources.

Search Engine Marketing (SEM)

Without waiting months and years to move up the ranking on search SERPs, you can choose the other way. The other way is always paid which is search engine marketing (SEM) or PPC. You can pay the search engine to show your ad at the top of the SERP. You need to spend your marketing budget on it and sometimes the target word becomes so costly that you just need to leave the idea of SEM. This is the type of advertising online that you pay once someone clicks your ad. It could be text or other forms of media. It's the most common type of ad on the internet.

Content Marketing through Blogging

The most important way you can market your business online is to build a blog. A blog is a place where you can post and share high-quality content that adds an exceedingly high amount of value to your business/brand/product. It's a long-term strategy and won't pay off overnight but every entrepreneur should understand the importance of embracing this online marketing method. A blog is also a necessary tool for creating authority. This authority will help you to attract the attention of consumers, the media and business owners alike.

Content Marketing on Medium and Quora

Both Quora & Medium are good places to get some early traffic in your new domain. Write one high-quality piece of content on your website which is keyword-centric, insightful, unique and adds a lot of value. Then go to authority sites like Quora or Medium and create another article there and add one link from that article using a primary or relevant keyword back to your website. It's called content marketing and it's a great way to speed up the ranking process and reach large existing audiences.

LinkedIn Connection

As a new Entrepreneur, you should never forget to ensure your existence at LinkedIn. It's a great way to quickly connect with others in your industry or niche. You can promote your business at LinkedIn and add value to your brand. Important information and ideas can also be shared here.

Facebook Ads

For any business and brand, Facebook is a great place to get both audience and customers. Facebook ads are not free, but it offers a great opportunity for reaching the right demographic for your business. You also use different metrics like interests, geographic location, marital status, age, and many others to locate potential audiences and customers.

Instagram Influencer Marketing

Social media lets you instantly reach droves of people from across the world at a moment's notice. Instagram is also an option but building up an audience base here is time-consuming and needs a lot of resources. The best to reach many followers and attract them is to hire Instagram Influencers. It will help you spread your business or brand to a vast majority of people easily.

Video Tutorials on YouTube

For any entrepreneur, presence at YouTube comes after ensuring your presence at Facebook. Since both Google & YouTube are under the same company, it's a great source to spread your brand and get traffic. You can do it by creating a

YouTube channel and creating useful video tutorials. Again, adding value should be your main concern. Be sure to drop a link inside the video description so that people can find your website easily.

Email Marketing

Email is probably the best way to generate ROI and it's also easy to use. There are tons of free email marketing tools that are available on the internet. Pick any one of them, and start communicating via email. You can get email addresses via newsletter subscription or other sources. Email can also be a great source for the brand image. Almost all successful entrepreneurs are using email marketing to spread their brand and business.

Angie's list or TripAdvisor

Different sites like Angie's list and TripAdvisor are a great source for any business to reach an enormous audience of potential customers. If your business if selling services don't forget to try Angie's List and if it's travel-related, the best place is TripAdvisor. These sites are a great place for links which will help you for SEO and a great place to get direct reviews from your customers.

Rich Snippets, AMP and FBIA

Rich snippets, Accelerated Mobile Pages (AMP) or Facebook Instant Articles (FBIA) are great sources for your business or brand to get some early exposure. These are easy to use and you just need to add some plugins to your website. You can get some traffic as well as potential customers via rich snippets, AMP and FBIA. Search Engines also encourages websites to use rich snippets by pushing them up to the SERP.

Forums

The forum is a great place to meet with industry leaders to spread your business and brand. Join conversations, chat with others, make suggestions, answer questions & add value to your business/brand. You will also be able to generate traffic from these forums as well as spread your business among your industry related people.

Digital Press Release

The press release is a great tool to spread your business, brand, and product. For any new business, you need to tell the public that you are here. People still spend a considerable amount of times reading the newspaper, and a press release can attract their attention. Press release posted online should consist of a link back to your website. This backlink is useful for SEO and can generate traffic to your site.

Social Media Viral Marketing

As a new entrepreneur, your presence at social media is important as well as using these social platforms to spread your business/brand is also crucial. Pinterest, Flickr, Tumblr & Instagram are high-domain authority sites, and you can post photos, videos to build up a follower base. Always use relevant hashtags and descriptions which will properly categorize your posting. These won't bring instant sales, but you will get a steady flow of traffic as well as an audience base. Don't forget to engage with others.

Now that you're familiar with that, you understand how marketing work on the internet. There are other forms of online marketing but these are just an overview of a few common online marketing strategies. Social media sites like

Facebook, LinkedIn, Reddit and Instagram offers PPC paid ads services as well. But, if you want to build a long-term fanbase, your best strategy is to combine paid ads with search engine optimization for long term results. Using social media is also a great way to reach your target audience in no time. You can use an Instagram account, Facebook page or even a Twitter handle to directly promote your business.

The marketing strategy you choose depends on your niche and target audience. Although Adwords ads are effective, promoting an image dependent brand like fashion or fitness will perform better on Instagram.

Your business is not a big-corporation with millions of dollars to spend on advertising. So, in your plan, include your intended marketing strategy too. More in-depth details for online marketing strategies will be given in future books.

Evaluate Your Marketing Efforts

Just simply getting your business started won't be enough. You have to monitor your marketing strategies on a regular basis. Focus on what's working and making sales, ditch anything that isn't. This is an area where you will have to do some research, don't worry it's not as difficult as it sounds.

All successful products need healthy marketing campaigns. A good place to start is to use modeling. Modeling is when you clone a successful existing business. Just go to Clickbank, Amazon or eBay and profile some successful businesses.

This involves...

1. Finding someone who is at the top of their niche.

2. Looking closely at their website and product.

3. Type the name of the product into the search engines and find out which review websites they are listed with. This will help you see the bigger picture.

4. Model your product and marketing around similar methods which have obviously proven to work.

Never be afraid to ask for help. Contact people, ask questions, learn and test things out.

Your Competition are Not Enemies, They are Allies

The more people know about your business, the more likely you will make regular sales. A proven way to spread the word is use the competition for promotion.

In order to do this, you should create an affiliate program. An affiliate program is a great way to leverage someone else's marketing efforts for your product; in return, you offer them a percentage of the price. At this point, you might be thinking that there's no way I'm giving up 50% to 60% of my profits to someone else. "I've done all the hard work why should I give up my profits". This is a natural way of thinking in the beginning, but it is wrong and flawed in many ways.

Imagine having a silent workforce working for you on autopilot day and night around the world, generating sales and doing marketing for you. What price would you put on that? These affiliates are your allies and they will make you a ton of money if you offer them good incentives. To put it into perspective lets look at an example...

Product "A" sells for $100, it has a great website and 800 mailing list subscribers. The seller of product A makes 10 sales a week = $1000.

The entrepreneur has no re-sellers or affiliate program set up. So visitors to his site only have the option to buy not re-sell the product. The businessperson gets all his buyers purely through direct marketing efforts.

While product "B" also sells for $100, it has a great website with 800 subscribers on their mailing list. The seller of product B makes 10 sales a week himself =$1000. However, he also has 10 re-sellers and an affiliate program set up offering 50% commission on each sale. His re-sellers make between 20 extra sales a week on top of his 10 sales which is = $1500: plus, visitors to his site have the option to buy and re-sell his product so his business is expanding all the time. He is getting a lot more traffic to his site than seller of product A because his affiliates are sending their traffic and subscribers over. So in effect, seller B is getting 10 times more traffic and 50% more profit than seller A.

If you have a large e-commerce store, you can create your own affiliate program. But, if you're selling a single product or service, it's best to use affiliate handlers.

Putting It All Together

Yes, it's easier to succeed online than it was 10 years ago. Still, you need to work hard at it to make the most impact. From the research planning, implementation, and marketing: you need to continuously keep an upbeat attitude about the possible outcomes. Don't fall for the myth that if you build it they will come. And don't invest all you have in creating a business no one will buy from. Knowledge is power only if you do the right things. Never be too busy to do your own research: try, learn and keep trying.

SECTION FOUR:

FOUNDATIONS OF SUCCESS

CHAPTER 8

Habits

"Your beliefs become your thoughts. Your thoughts make your words, your words make your actions, your actions become your habits, your habits make your values and your values become your destiny." - **Mahatma Gandhi**

Positive thinking and a positive self-image are the foundations of any successful person. Although the words of Mahatma Gandhi were spoken in a different time and a different context but, yet they are absolutely true. Your thinking about yourself will be the product of your life. If you desire a positive, healthy and successful life: then think in like manner.

Stephen R. Covey, author of "The Seven Habits of Highly Effective People", outlined 7 habitual actions that successful people have that the Average Joe does not.

These habits are:

- Be positive

- Begin with the end in mind

- Put first things first

- Think win-win

- Seek first to understand,

- Then to be understood you need to synergize

- Practice what you know

Positive thinking helps you to effectively manage stress and improves your health. Your personality, mental health, and the results you see are built on your opinion about situations in your life whether positive or negative.

Research has shown that personality traits, such as optimism and pessimism can affect one's health and well-being. Positive thinking is a major strategy for effective stress management. Thinking positively does not mean that you will ignore life's challenges, but instead, it means being positive in your approach to handling these challenges productively. When you stay for long periods in a high spirit, you reduce stress and build up resistance against confrontational situations.

Conversely, if you feel bad about yourself, you are sad and see nothing good about you: your stress level increases. Depleting you of your power to overcome challenges.

Positive thinking is medicine to the body, mind, and soul. If you are mentally alert and active, your body will also be: it will generate more resistance to stress and produce more positive vibes.

Positive thinking is so powerful that it helps you overcome your limitations. When you stop focusing on your excuses, your mind starts revealing solutions to the problem.

As you venture on your success journey, there are certain areas of life you need to pay attention to. Ignoring them may lead to dire consequences. Your health, relationships, business ethics and personal finances are the four major aspects of reality you must not ignore. Or else, you pay the ultimate price.

Health

It is known that you can get sick when you keep on saying you are sick in like manner, you can also talk yourself into a better health.

This may sound strange, but I believe that if you have a health problem, thinking positively and visualizing a healthy, strong body will help you to get better, you will heal faster, and the level of sickness in your body will decrease.

Thinking positively gives strength to the body. It has been discovered from scientific research that a positive self-image, positive thinking and speaking positive words consistently: enables the body to heal faster and build up more resistance against diseases.

This is important because you don't want to sacrifice your health for success. You don't have to do that. You can have it all if you truly believe and manage your time properly. Pay attention to what you eat. Try to fit at least 2 hours of weekly exercise into your schedule. Go for routine check-ups.

Maintaining your health goes beyond diseases: how you feel, and handle stress greatly affects your productivity levels. Each time you notice yourself feeling weak, take a break. Go for a walk or visit family. Never stay in isolation for too long. That stuff will mess you up.

Relationships

Having a right attitude is the key to a more close, fulfilling and successful relationship with your partner or colleagues. It's difficult to be around someone who complains about everything they can find. Likewise, you will attract others to yourself if you say positive things about yourself, what you do, and the people around you.

There are several principles upon which relationships are established. When couples keep on saying positive things about each other, their relationship is strengthened, and more love is stirred up in their hearts towards one another.

Staying positive serves as a glue that will strengthen your relationships with your partner, family, friends, colleagues, and even your boss.

Business

Which do you think is better if you want to have a good relationship with your partners, colleagues, and customers?

Complaining and saying negative things continuously: or speaking positive, constructive and challenging remarks? Obviously, you choose the latter because the former will destroy your business.

Successful entrepreneurs are people with a positive self-image and positive attitude. They are the ones who are willing and ready to do anything necessary to achieve their goals. The ethics of your online business is important: you don't want to supercharge after an angry customer feedback on Twitter. A positive mindset helps you leverage such events as an opportunity to grow and improve.

Finance

What are your thoughts about money? Do you think it's scarce or there's abundance? Your words make visible what you are thinking. Anytime you say you don't have money, it simply means that you have focused your energy and your belief on not having money, then you begin to experience money problems.

Your attitude towards money will change when you begin to have a positive thought towards it. If you think and talk more positively about money, then you are telling the whole world that you are happy to receive it.

Being an entrepreneur does not automatically fix a bad money mindset. Ever heard of PewdiePie, yes, the YouTube gaming sensation. He became a millionaire by uploading videos of himself playing games online. Like how easy is that? There are babies earning millions of dollars online doing unboxing videos.

What is your reason for thinking money is scarce? Money is literally everywhere. You only need the right mindset and positioning to attract it your way. Positive thinking triggers enthusiasm: your mind opens, and you begin to see solutions, instead, of only the negative events.

Only you have the power to control your thoughts, nobody can do it for you. Discover this power and exercise it to encourage yourself in focusing on more positive things.

You can control what enters your mind and what you think about. But because we have been accustomed to negativity in our experiences of life; therefore, we tend to focus our minds on the negative areas than the positive ones.

Building your online empire requires investment. You could get people to invest in your ideas. If you have a bad attitude and terrible money management skills, you can't grow your business. Success won't happen overnight. You need to manage what you currently have especially if you're a solopreneur with no job to fall back on, partners, or savings. You can get what you desire but, take small steps if you can't afford the risk. I know you've heard it a thousand times: take the big risk they say. If you can't afford such, you are better off moving one step at a time. It will take you more time to get there, still, it's better than jumping into the shark tank unprotected. The height of your goals is irrelevant once you realize that even the farthest distance can be reached if you move step by step.

Having a positive self-image, positive thought and a positive view of the entire world will enable you to consciously achieve more goals, have more thrilling relationships, better health, and fitness. You will attain whatever you dream of but never ignore your wellbeing. You need money to survive, good food to fuel your body, people to rely on and positive ethics to foster your business relationships.

SECTION FIVE:

THE POWER OF WORDS

CHAPTER 9

Brand Yourself

Words are powerful: they are effective agents of change we use to influence ourselves and others. Using the right words determines how people perceive your brand.

The word "green" evokes a sustainable and natural image in people's mind. "Sales" on the other hand refers to cheap, even if it's not. We associate certain feelings with particular words. That is why you need to describe your brand with the right words. Think of the emotions you want people to associate with your business. You can also add your product, niche, or service to your name. This creates a clear picture of what you do.

Beyond that, the everyday words you use on your business social media platform, website, blog or product description also contribute significantly to your brand perception.

Your Words, Your Reality

The words you use daily to describe yourself, business and people around you impact your reality. The right words will shape your mind towards the path of success. You'll meet the right people and you will feel better about yourself. Most people are accustomed to negative words. We swear, curse and complain: we never seem to have a short supply of negative self-demeaning words. Speaking positively, however, is a skill that you need to practice. Remember that negativity is the natural state. You need to deliberately try towards cleaning your mind of the words that hold you back from reaching your full potential.

Top 30 Words for a Positive Mind Revolution

When you first start using the words listed below, it will seem senseless and ridiculous. Through continuous practice, it will not only reset your mind positively, your energy rises instantly: and others will also give a positive reaction towards you as you discuss with them.

Don't just learn it, use these words in your everyday conversations and see how it will impact positively on your life.

Here are 30 words that can help you combat your negative thoughts:

- Absolutely

- Best

- Amazing

- Exceptional

- Abundant

- Glorious

- Deluxe

- Dynamic

- Abundance

- Dependable

- Optimistic

- Appealing

- Energetic

- Distinctive

- Immaculate

- Outstanding

- Inspiring

- Resourceful

- Incredible

- Finest

- Passionate

- Calm

- Exciting

- Wonderful

- Effortless

- Divine

- Generous

- Fantastic

- Adore

- Excellent

Understanding the Growth Terminology

When you listen to Zig Ziglar's tape on How to be a winner, you will realize that the outcomes of our lives are dependent on the motivations we get from our environment. We wake up with the sound of the alarm clock beeping.

When people most times wake up with alarms, it creates fear and a sense of inadequacy in them because they failed to regulate their sleep cycle: they often become negative. Now, how do you expect to have a positive day when you start your day wrong? Some of us say words like "I hate" the first thing in the morning. This is going to affect how you feel. You can't hate your customers no matter how annoying some of them may be. Use the right phrases and sentences to start right and finish strong.

Grant Cardone, a real estate sales guy, author and motivational speaker: expand this point. He never invests in anything that won't make him money for sure. Notice that word there "for sure", it defines the entire sentence. This is what happens when you speak to people. Using strong assertive words with a positive tune to create a clear image of what you desire. Regardless of whether you are speaking to yourself, customers, partners, investors, family, or strangers: be real with your statements.

Don't beat around the corners. Say Yes when you want to and No if you don't want to give in to a request. Avoid open statements and dialogues, commit to your schedule. Positive assertive terminology impacts your mind, feelings, and actions.

It is what you say that will become your reality: so, instead of using negative or week phrases in your speeches use positive assertive words to replace them. This will increase your motivation and help you get better results.

When you start talking about yourself and about things around you in a positive way and with a light heart; your mind becomes open to receive new ideas, and you will react to tough situations in a more excellent and stress-free manner.

CHAPTER 10

Question Everything

Questions are very essential if you really want to improve your positive thinking. Whenever you encounter a problem, if you could activate positive ideas and affirmation within you, you will surely get a solution.

Instead of making up your mind that it is impossible, or you begin to feel you can't do it: rephrase the problem before you into a question. A clear example is How can I...?' Or what do I need to do to...?

Whenever you ask your mind questions, it automatically starts searching for an answer. Your mind was not built to think unless there are questions bothering you.

Even if you don't speak the answers to the questions, your mind will still do its work by providing the answer or continue searching until it does.

Take note of the type of questions you ask yourself because it determines the type of answer you'll get.

For instance, if you ask yourself 'why I can't get a girlfriend?!' – Your mind will answer you with something like 'Because you are stupid or ugly'. And honestly this is not the kind of answer you are expecting, but it comes to you like that. Instead, try to change the type of question in a more positive way, like these:

How can I find the love of my life'?

What do I need to do to accomplish my dream?

How can I tackle this challenge best?

What can I do to improve myself on this area?

As you can see, these questions target a solution. They are framed in such a way that your mind will search for an answer that points out the solution, instead of providing answers that reduces your self-image, your self-esteem, your confidence and your positive attitude.

Questions also help you define the reason why you do what you do. It clarifies and simplifies your reality in the way that only powerful thinking can.

Persuade with Words

Any time we use powerful words in written messages, it emphasizes more and has a deeper impact. The right words make customers click.

But more importantly, it persuades your subconscious mind. Writing small positive statements on papers and putting it in some strategic places where you can see it daily: empowers you to feel more energetic and focused to do everything you need to do.

Seeing the sticky notes on your wall may seem ridiculous at first: but once you get comfortable, you'll imagine how you ever lived without it. You'll get used to it and it feels great too. Persuasive words are crucial to your personal and business success. These words empower action. The most notable of them are:

- Me – because you are the most important person in the world.

- Mine – you own your reality.

- How – sparkes your creativity.

- New – entails your innovative potentials.

- Who – identify the right people.

- Money – is the ultimate tool to attain your dream lifestyle.

- Now – what can you do now that will make the most difference tomorrow.

- People – how are you treating those in your circle and vice versa.

- Why – your motivation starts here.

These words are also important for creating your brand and marketing strategy for your internet venture. Everyone wants to feel special, involved and motivated. Whenever you speak with anyone, you either influence yourself or the person you are meeting influence you: and in rare cases you both influence yourselves.

Using these words makes your persuasion efforts more successful. People will listen to you more and pay attention to your business.

These words are very useful in whatever you are offering whenever you start marketing to your audience. Another great advantage of these words is that you can use them to present your goals in a more specific and more powerful way. Remember that attainable goals are necessary to become more successful, more focused, more optimistic, and create more self-esteem and self-confidence.

Whenever you are talking or thinking, use positive words such as, 'I can', 'I am able', 'it is possible', 'it can be done', etc

In your conversations, use words that arouse feelings and mental images of strength, happiness and success.

SECTION SIX:
NAVIGATING YOUR FEELINGS

CHAPTER 11

Changing Your Thinking Patterns

When you change the way you feel, your thinking pattern will change from mediocre into positive.

Your reality about the perception of situations can also be transformed when you change the way you act or react to it. There is no true or false in how you perceive things but focus on the best results possible in every situation.

Develop an attitude of feeling good about yourself, feeling optimistic, challenged, enthusiastic, motivated, encouraged, passionate and compelled. So that you can generate a motion of positive vibes throughout your body, that creates a neuro-chemical reaction, called endorphins.

Endorphins are the body's own produced chemicals that you feel when you're feeling fantastic. Such as the feeling you have when you are in a rollercoaster-ride, with the people you love or eating your favorite food.

This kind of feeling at those special moments promotes your positive thinking. You can never feel bad or have negative thoughts when you are experiencing feelings of ecstasy.

The question now is: how do you increase your good feelings? – well, that's easier than you think – all you need to do is decide how you want to feel good about yourself. It's mostly a matter of choice to feel either good or bad about yourself. Unless you lost someone close to you, experiencing medical situations or a disaster: you can allow yourself to feel positivity.

How to Change Your Feeling at Any Moment

Whenever you think back on moments and situations that have made you excited, happy and felt good about life: you recall this feeling of excitement in you which makes you see a reason why you need to be happy again.

Do you still have that exciting picture in your mind?

Yeah!!!

Okay, then, visualize it.

Bring back the feelings you had during those exciting periods. Make sure they are positive feelings. Try to locate where you are having those feelings in your body, for example, you could be happy when you felt like butterflies were flying in your stomach. Then connect to the feeling by putting your hands on your stomach. Enlarge the feelings, down to your legs and your toes and up again to your chest and your face then to your head.

Do you feel that? Great!

Now, you can make this feeling more intense and more powerful. Make sure you overwhelm yourself with this feeling of positivity: you will feel wonderful every time you do this exercise.

Impulsive Emotions

In 1960, a scientific research was conducted to detect how emotional impact was transmitted. It showed that 90% of the way we feel is transmitted through the impulses we receive from our body through the brain, movements of our body parts and from the tone of our voice.

This means that the way you speak to yourself or to someone else and how you communicate with your body will have a great impact in achieving your goals and your level of self-esteem.

If you yell forceful and fearful words, your subconsciousness and probably some other persons listening to you will receive the information as being aggressive and attacking. As a positive thinker, you should always see encouraging thoughts before you act. Doing so impacts not how you feel but how other people react to you. Smile before calling a difficult person.

Think happy thoughts when you're describing your business. Stand upright, use your assertive voice and expect optimistic replies when you make a post online or start a conversation with someone.

Change the Negative Triggers

The way you feel is based on how you think of yourself and your feelings are programmed from the moment you were born.

Whenever you associate yourself with a certain event, your brain connects a particular feeling with that event. For example, when you were young, and you needed to go to the doctor for the first time, you probably didn't have any clue what was going to happen. You trusted him and when he said that 'this isn't going to hurt' when he gave you the anti-flu shot, you believed him. In fact, it did hurt. You then associated that experience with pain and insincerity.

The next time you saw a doctor; you were probably more careful to trust his words. If the doctor would say 'Don't worry, this isn't going to hurt' again, an automatic trigger would arise and make you suspicious if he was telling the truth.

The more often an event triggers certain emotion, the stronger the association becomes and the longer it takes to change that trigger. However, the positive side of this story is that it's not impossible to change your triggers. Whatever your experiences were in the past, they don't have to be in front of you every time a similar event takes place in the present.

The past doesn't equal the present or the future. Connecting new feeling to an event, and repeatedly practicing and strengthening that emotion, manifests in a new neurological network in your brain.

You can literally change your thinking patterns. Think and feel happy, comforting, optimistic, encouraging, motivating, loving thoughts and connect to the feelings that come along. If you have any difficulties with feeling good feelings, you can imagine yourself in a situation in which you were feeling fantastic. As if you were on top of the world. This is called visualizing. Visualizing works for everyone.

You can connect to a feeling by thinking of something, seeing pictures, hearing nice sounds or even smelling or tasting something positive in your mind's eyes. Your senses are directly linked to your most powerful neurological network and they store memories you collected throughout your life. Remember, humans are emotional beings. Allow into your awareness only feelings of happiness, strength and success.

Your Voice Say More Than the Words You Speak

When you think the thoughts you would like to think, feel the feelings you would like to feel, and use your voice in an active way: your words start to resonate with yourself.

Remember, it's all in how you say it that makes the difference. Try it out for a couple times, and you'll experience the difference for yourself. Change the pitch of your voice, from a low one to a higher one: you'll notice you command more respect as people start perceiving your authority more.

Low tonalities in your voice resonate easier with mediocre and negativity. On the other side, a higher, firmer tone of voice, establishes a more self-confident, positive and optimistic reflection of your thoughts.

Visualiaze Into Reality

There are two things the mind understands when spoken to. The first one is emotions or feelings. The other one is images or pictures. The mind is a very visual oriented part of the human body and it doesn't really understand the words that are spoken, rather than the mental pictures that are connected to them.

So, if you want something to change within yourself or the way you perceive something (or yourself), change the picture you see in your mind's eye.

Visualization is one of the most powerful tools that you can use on a daily basis to transform your life and attract success.

Some people say that they can't visualize, but that's not true. Everyone has an imagination, you just need to learn how to use it more.

Open Your Mind to Your Dreams

Exercise:

- Take a couple of seconds to relax. Breathe in slowly and exhale at a calm pace. Do this a couple times. This ensures you to open up your mind and step out of the hectics of daily life.

  Now, close your eyes and take a couple more breaths. Think back of your house you live in right now. Maybe you see it as a general picture, maybe in specifics. Now, zoom in a little on your front door. What color does it has? What is it made of? Where is the handle? Are there any specific markings on the door, such as a nameplate, a sticker or even a mailbox slit? Try to make it as detailed as possible by focusing on your front door only.

What you just did, is visualization. It's a mental picture you made in your mind about something. Now visualization works not only for your eyes. You can use visualization also with your touch, your hearing, even your smell and your taste. Before deciding to implement your plans, visualize your outline clearly in your mind seeing it succeed. If you visualize with concentration and faith, you will be amazed at the results.

The Strategy that Works Every Time

There's a simple formula that you can remember to help you think more positive on a conscious level. It's the event plus your response that causes the outcome of a situation.

$$E + R = O \longrightarrow EVENT + RESPONSE = OUTCOME$$

Since the event itself doesn't change, it's the way you perceive information about the event and the way you respond that determines the result.

Example: Someone comes to you shouting (Event). You can decide to either yell back (Response) or to stay calm and see what is causing his action (Response). The choice you choose influences the next action of that person (Outcome). If you shout back, the chances are that you end up in a verbal fight and the situation can quickly escalate into a physical fight. But, the second option will help you understand the situation better. You just might make him your friend.

Now, this may seem as a corny example, but imagine this person is the best friend, or a family member, or your partner. No one can push your buttons unless you allow them to. You cannot control what happens to you, but your reaction is determined by your decision.

CHAPTER 12

Directed Perception and Procedure

It's the way you guide your mind's thoughts that influence your perception of the situation. What are you focusing on? What kind of result do you want? Do you want something better? Then change your perception. Changing your perception can be very difficult especially when you are not alone.

- For example, you come home from a long day's work to your partner and you need some attention. You just want your partner to remind you that he or she loves you. If your partner is very busy and didn't notice you, you might lose your optimism and feel rejected.

This is the result of the event, based upon your response, or in this case your partner's inaction. It's the way you perceived the situation and responded to it, that resulted the change of emotions.

"Awaken the Giant Within" by Tony Robbins explains that you can change two things to ensure your desired result. Those two things are, either change your perception or your procedure. Meaning you can change the way you perceive the event by understanding why it happened in the first place. Why is no one responding to your online post? Why are your followers ignoring your brand? Think of the other person's perspective. Taking a different point of view usually clarifies a lot.

By stepping out of your comfort zone and into other people's views, you'll see that you'll understand much more why the others react the way they do.

The other way to influence the outcome is to change your procedure. This means that you can change your way of interacting with the other person. Learn to notice other people's emotional response and adjust accordingly.

- Don't ask people difficult questions or request for a favor when they are in a bad mood. Wait for a while, when you see that the situation have become more relaxed, go for what you wanted to ask or say.

By changing your approach, you may create a different result than, otherwise, anticipated. It's your action that is reacted upon by others: remember that it is what you can control.

CHAPTER 13

<hr />

The Silent Power of Self-talk

Most people won't admit it, but almost everybody talks to themselves. Most of the time we don't even notice it because it's happening so unconsciously that we hardly pay attention to it.

But how many times have you stood in front of the mirror, boosting your self-esteem by telling yourself that you were looking absolutely fabulous. This is self-talk: it reflects how we feel, your perception and self-esteem. But rather than letting circumstances determine how you should feel, you can decide what to say to yourself. You can positively impact your self perception, the situations and your day as you want with little pep talks.

If you want to have a better self-image, then use positive words when you speak to yourself. Talk to yourself in a manner that shows you are proud of who you are and what you do. Even when you don't feel like doing it at first, the repetition will persuade your subconscious mind into start believing that you truly love your reality.

- You could start of by saying simple words or phrases like "I'm willing to see the opportunities of today" or "Today something wonderful is going to happen to me" or "I like myself more every day".

Be sure to involve your feelings as you speak: It's not the words itself that will make the change on your subconscious. Because if you say a phrase like "I like myself more every day" in a flattened, low energy kind of tone, your subconscious mind will reply you sarcastically saying "Yeah, right! Who're you trying to fool?"

You can use words to influence how you feel, the way you see yourself and, thus, your results. You can harness the full potential of self-talk by also adding visualization and body movements. See yourself as the person you want to be. Believe that you are already there. Tell yourself how you'll handle a difficult situation when the time arises.

Positive thinking relates to many more things than just thinking happy thoughts at certain times of the day. Create a positive self-image of your self in your mind, see it and start acting accordingly. Believe in your own vision of who you are to a fault. It's not going to change overnight, but it's essential in changing your self-perception mindset and strengthening it towards the positive ones.

Most people's negative self-image developed as they grew. Whether it's in our culture, the way we were raised by our parents or the economic times: it's been proven over and over again that an optimistic self-image is necessary to achieve massive success. You can't stand in front of millions of people to give a speech if you think you are trash. Your mind will tell you no one wants to hear what you have to say. You may be an expert on the topic, but once this thought comes along, you'll think less of yourself.

It takes longer to change negative thought into positive ones than if the situation is reversed. The data shows that on average, it takes three to five times more positivity to 'overwrite' one negativity.

Headlines like "90% of all businesses fail in their first five years of existence" can damage your confidence: you may subconsciously delay or even dismiss starting or growing your online business to its fullest potential. Don't bother with these negative facts, you will get to your destination if you persist.

According to Tony Robbins, there are three things you can do right now to instantly boost your self-image. This triad affects how you feel, act and think.

Transform Your Reality with Body Movements

The first one is to focus on your physiology.

The way your body tells you and others how you feel, isn't something that you consciously control, but it's something that is connected with the state of mind. If you focus and listen, you will detect it.

- Exercise:

When you experience something unpleasant like anxiety, your body immediately changes the posture to match that mind-state.

You might lower your shoulders, drop your head a little or cross your arms or legs. The same physiology works when you have a positive feeling like excitement. Your body starts to stretch, you stand tall, your head is upward and you probably smile too.

Your mind cannot differentiate what is imagined from reality. So, your visible body reaction is always affected by what is happening in your head.

If you consciously change your physiology from a head down, shoulders down, low energy posture to a face forward, head straight, shoulders back, smiling or focused posture: your self-image and the thoughts connected to that image will change positively.

Transform Your Self-perception Through Focus

In addition to your physiology, the events, situations, feelings or thoughts you're focusing on will determine how you perceive yourself. If you focus on happy thoughts, as a logical consequence your behavior, your attention and your self-image will change towards the positive.

Now it may sound a bit superficial that just by changing your focus, your self-image will change as well. But Abraham Lincoln, someone who was considered all but superficial said "people are just about as happy as they made up their minds to be".

What you focus on the most results in how you see yourself and how you feel during that specific time. It comes down to this: you have the choice to be happy or unhappy; to be negative or positive oriented. The question becomes, What do you want to focus on today?

Say It Like You Mean It

Language is the final part that completes the triad of how your behavior affects your self-image. Words are so powerful, that they can literally make you ill.

If you'd say 'I'm not good enough' or I'm not worth it' or 'I can't do this', your mind, spirit, and body will automatically transfer this information into your subconscious. It's as if your language is the input of your own supercomputer mind.

On the bright side, realizing this creates the opportunity to start changing your self-image by speaking in a positive and constructive way to yourself and to others. You see, the reason we use communication is basically set on two reasons: 1) to convince or to influence other people, and 2) to influence or convince ourselves. Of course, a combination of both is also possible (e.g. in a discussion or debate).

So, if you want to change your own perception (or the perception and/or energy of someone else), focus on the kind of language you use. Speak of positive and empowering words:

- Say it to yourself while smiling:

'I can do this', 'I'm committed to feeling better every day', 'I'm valuable', 'I love myself more every time I look in the mirror', 'it's going to be a great day for opportunities'

The more often you use this type of language, the easier it will become and the better it will work for you. The power of language is an undervalued skill. Practice your self-talk and soon you'll notice massive changes in your vocabulary.

SECTION SEVEN:

HOW SUCCESSFUL PEOPLE DO IT

CHAPTER 14

Habits

Successful people achieve successes because of their self-perception, their thought patterns, and how they act. Their habits align with their thoughts. Successful people have successful habits.

When the average person thinks about achieving their goals, they envision some big breakthrough moment, that's very far from the truth. Those who rise to the top of their niches focus on the small seemingly insignificant actions they take each day. It's not about the one who takes 1000 steps a day, but the person who moves one step towards his goals 1000 times. Consistency is key: it's hard to learn. You can't fool your brain as old habits die hard.

Your brain is designed for efficiency. It won't allow you spend energy on what is unimportant to you. Your subconscious mind needs repetition to transform itself. Your best strategy for achieving your goals is to use good habits.

We all have habits, the actions we find ourselves taking without our conscious control. Alcoholics have a habit of drinking, smokers have the habit of lighting up: and, unsuccessful people have a habit of giving up too early. You are a sum of your habits: we form these behaviors by repeating the cue, action, and reward cycle. You get triggered by an image, sound, or thought: you act then get rewarded by your brain with feel-good chemicals.

It's not an accident that most CEOs and Founders wake up at 5:00 am, they practiced this behavior until it became a habit. What is the first thing you do in the morning? What patterns have you noticed in your life? Are they supportive of your goals or limit you? Think about that. If you've always insulted people who disagree with you online, there's a high tendency that you'll repeat the same behavior with potential customers who piss you off.

The Top 10 Habits of Successful People

- They look for and find opportunities where others see nothing.

- They strategically create their own success, while others hope success will find them.

- They are fearful like everyone else, but they are not controlled or limited by fear.

- They ask the right questions

- They maximize their potential.

- They align themselves with like-minded people.

- They actually visualize and plan.

- They are life-long learners.

- They take calculated risks.

- They are adaptable and embrace change.

Build Powerful Habits Through Routines

When Dwayne Johnson was asked how he managed to get an insane amount of workout done while filming: he replied that he has a very strict routine of waking up four hours early before he needed to be on set. The reason he can do this is that our minds create habits of the things we do repeatedly, so we can be more effective.

Your brain knows that if you think about everything you want to do, you'll never act. It automates the tasks, so the subconscious mind can take over. The actions we take repeatedly becomes natural to us.

You too can use routines in your life to keep you motivated, get things done faster and accomplish your goals.

Here are 7 routines every day that will greatly improve your life:

- **Showering**

Sound too simple to even be on this list but it's a very important ritual that some of us ignore. Taking a shower every morning ignites your mind and body. No matter how limited your time is, never forget to take a nice and rejuvenating shower in the morning before leaving the house and another at night to relax you for bed. *Extra tip*: 2 or 3 mornings a week, try a 15-20 second cold shower just before you hop out.

- **Get a Sleep Pattern**

You should not sacrifice too much sleep to achieve your goals. Humans can survive 21 days without food or water, but, 10 days without sleep and you'll be dead.

Sleep is a very important part of our biology, that is why you should at least manage it. You need to create a sleep pattern that works for you. Most people are deprived of quality sleep – the most effective way to achieve better sleep is by using a pattern. This means going to bed and waking up at the same time every day. Also, waking up early is crucial to your success because your brain's performance is at its peak and your willpower is fully charged in the morning. When you wake up early, you have more hours to get things done before you lose motivation for the day.

- **Stop Complaining**

Complaining focuses your mind on the problem, and you miss out on opportunities to improve the situation. Blaming the situation or other people makes the problem worse, not better. There will be times when you do everything right and still don't succeed: but if you remember you control your reaction, you won't waste time complaining.

Steve Jobs was bullied out of his own company. You know what he did next? He bought Pixar. He could have given up and said maybe this entrepreneurship thing is not for me but No, he moved on.

Life is full of ups and downs: there's no way one can control everything that happens to them, you can only manage your reactions. Having a proactive mindset protects you from the pitfalls you will stumble upon. When you complain, you can't see the future opportunities for growth. Besides, nobody wants to be with a negative person: negativity spreads like the flu. Stop complaining, look on the positive side of things, and you'll attract amazing like-minded people. If you desire more of the finer things in life, then practice saying all the things that you are grateful for every morning.

- **Prepare Before Bed**

Writing down your goals for the next day before bed the previous night keeps your brain alert. Remember during your high school days, whenever you prepared for a test or a report deadline before bed, you tend to wake up earlier than usual. This happened because preparing ahead before bed creates an internal alarm.

To do this, find a quiet place to relax your mind and write down your goals every evening. Make sure to keep your list simple.

- **Workout and Eat Healthy**

You simply cannot attain wealth without taking care of your health. The practices of the food industry have made it difficult for us to get the nourishment our bodies need. Your best bet is to give up the junk food, focus on eating whole natural foods.

Ever heard of the phrase health is wealth? You need your body and mind to be nourished for success. Eating junk food makes you lazy and deprives you of the joy of life. Your brain cannot perform at its peak if you keep feeding it with unhealthy foods. The best diet is a balanced diet full of healthy fats, organic fruit and vegetables and lean proteins.

Spend some time at the gym and be active, your body needs the energy. Food is too important for your survival for you to be passive about it.

Make time to plan what you'll eat during the week so that you're not caught off guard. Because if you fail to plan your meals ahead, you will find it much more challenging to make healthy choices when you are hungry. This is not just about losing or maintaining weight, it's about your physical and mental wellbeing.

- "Challenge is the pathway to engagement and progress in our lives. But not all challenges are created equal. Some challenges make us feel alive, engaged, connected, and fulfilled. Others simply overwhelm us. Knowing the difference as you set bigger and bolder challenges for yourself is critical to your sanity, success, and satisfaction" - **Brendon Burchard**

Living a healthy life is a challenge that we must engage in. You can't give up: your body needs you to make the right choices. We are built to move: when we exercise, the brain release endorphins which are the feel-good chemicals that make us happy.

There's no special workout plan that is right for everyone. If running is not your thing, try swimming, cycling, or tennis: anything that makes you move intensely. No, Yoga does not count because it's a relaxation technique. You need to fire up those muscles, get your heart rate up and increase the blood flow to your brain.

If you're very busy and can't find time for the gym, everyone has 10 minutes in the morning to go for a walk, maybe some sprints. Choose the stairs, instead, of the escalator. If changing your office desk for a standing one appeals to you, then go for it. Whatever makes you move, find a way to do it. You'll improve your mood, sleep better, protect your brain and of course have a great looking body.

- **Enjoy the Moment**

This confuses a lot of people. Yes, you are aiming to achieve your goals, and you need to keep focused on them, but, that does not mean you should deprive yourself of the joys of the present.

Thinking too much of the future makes you worried and creates anxiety. Robert Kiyosaki, the "Rich Dad Poor Dad" guru describes being contented as when one is satisfied with the present but still looks forward to a better future. Meaning that while you are thinking and planning how to make your dreams come true, you should be conscious of what you already have.

Practice the mindful art of staying in the moment. When you learn to be in the present, you take a conscious step to teach your mind to focus on the now. This is why meditation is so beneficial, even if it's just 20 minutes daily it will improve your mood a lot.

Our minds are so used to wandering that if you truly want to produce positive results you should take steps to refocus your attention whenever you catch yourself drifting. Don't watch those mindless TV shows and waste your time on the couch, you can't sleepwalk through life and expect massive success. Life is not a passive endeavor, you need to participate. So, get off the sideline and become the star player in your own life.

- **Use Social Media Wisely**

Be honest with yourself, can you live without checking social media for a single day? I bet that just thinking about the question sends your heart racing because you know you've become addicted to social media.

Okay, it gets twisted here: you are an online entrepreneur, your success depends on your ability to engage people on social media, so, why do you need to avoid it?

Social media is a tool, and you need to use it in the right way or else it will deprive you of your productive time, focus, and money. Research shows social media is addictive because of the way the sites are designed: it's the people who make the sites that have found a way to hack our subconscious minds so that we'll continue using their products. Humans are social beings, we always seek to fit in and be accepted. This is why social media is so captivating for most of us. But, as an internet entrepreneur, you need to decide to take control of your mind and use social media for your benefit.

The simple strategy is to plan the time you spend online. Learn to avoid those impulsive moments when you feel bored and immediately pick up your phone to browse social media. Instead, schedule the time wisely: you can also inform your customers when you'll be available to answer their questions. If this doesn't work, then hire a virtual assistant.

Your extra time could be spent doing tasks that directly improve your life and business productivity. Remember, your time is the one thing that you can never get back.

CHAPTER 15

Goals

Success means different things to different people, what is unique is that everyone has an idea and vision of what our individual success is like. For some people, success is all about reaching a certain academic level, securing a well-paid job, building a desired career, buying their dream house and car. While to some others, success means finding the right partner, building a great family and watch their kids grow. In all, there is a need to set goals and work tirelessly towards it. It helps you determine what success means to you. Building an online empire is not your only goal in life; still, when you achieve it, it will make a huge difference in your life.

On your journey to achieving your dreams, things can get twisted. The only reason why those who conquer continue in their struggle is because they are goal-oriented. They constantly think of solutions to the obstacles they face. It's your goal that fire you up with motivation and perseverance to get what you really want.

Brian Tracy describe it this way "only losers don't know what they want, and therefore don't get what they want; it's winners who have a clear idea on what they want and who are willing to go for it".

Goal setting is an absolute must if you want to live the life you envision. If you don't set goals, you're bound to fail.

<u>The Art of Goal-setting</u>

Goal-setting is one of those things that seems like it should be very simple but can often cause anguish and aggravation. Even worse, if it's not done productively it can convince us that we're doomed to failure and prompt us to give up on our dreams forever.

The number one mistake that most people make when goal-setting is reaching too high right from the get-go. There is nothing wrong with aiming high – it's great. However, what most people fail to consider is the process of growth and development that must take place between where they begin and where they'd like to end up.

You would not expect an infant to set a goal to climb Mt. Everest, would you? Perhaps, later, when that infant has learned how to crawl and walk, and after he has grown into a man and strengthened his body and conditioned himself to deal with the harsh elements. And after he has tackled smaller and less dangerous mountains – yes. But not before the necessary growth, development and preparation have taken place.

Many people try to make a similar large leap when they set their goals. They want to transform themselves from a position of lack and fear to a position of power and success in the shortest period of time, and it's just not likely. It's not impossible: stranger things have happened, but let's just say it's very rare.

The good news is that every large goal can be broken down into smaller, more manageable goals. Even those steps can be broken down into smaller goals, such as buying some books or taking some classes to educate yourself on niche marketing; joining a gym, starting a healthy eating plan, etc.

Successful goal-setting is as easy as learning how to identify the mini-goals that compose each larger goal, and focusing your efforts on those first. That doesn't mean you can't keep your larger goal in mind and keep pushing yourself to reach it. However, giving most of your attention to the smaller steps along the journey will result in less stress and much quicker progress.

Take another look at the vision you wrote for your life, and then ask yourself how this big achievement might be broken down into smaller steps. If you can come up with some reasonable action steps you can take immediately, you will gain confidence with each small achievement you make. As your confidence grows and you gain experience and knowledge, your action steps will automatically become bigger and bolder, and so will your results.

It's okay to have an idea about when you will reach your goals because it can definitely keep you motivated and focused. But it can also backfire if you don't see results quickly enough and make you give up out of sheer impatience.

Be reasonable and balanced about your goals. Just like you can't expect to make a giant leap from "here" to "there", you also can't expect to accomplish everything overnight. There are two good ways to keep your goal-setting balanced:

- Focus on the sense of accomplishment you get from every step you take. Rather than pinning your satisfaction only on the big goal you have in mind, allow yourself to feel good about the progress you're making toward that goal. Feel proud about the great job you're doing and really allow yourself to enjoy the journey.

- Don't worry about the timeframe. This one is definitely more challenging, but it's also very freeing. Instead of setting a timeframe, simply commit to working steadily and enthusiastically on each small action step. Don't buy into impatience if you don't see results immediately – in fact, let the actions themselves be their own rewards. Feel good that you are strengthening your self-discipline and growing more completely into the person you were meant to be.

What Are You Willing to Give for Your Success?

Be aware that you need to pay the price for success. Every success always has a price that you need to pay, and you need to pay it in advance. It's these two factors that you absolutely need to consider, in order to be successful.

H.L. Hunt, an American oil tycoon, and business legend explain that to get to your dream you must:

- First, decide what you want. Many people don't get what they want because they don't know what they want. And this is why they don't succeed in life. Most people also want a lot of things in life, but not one thing in particular, and end up settling for far less than they're capable of.

- Second, if you established what it is you want, you need to be willing to pay the price for it. Every success comes at a price and you need to clarify how much you're willing to pay and then resolve to pay it.

The price for success is paid for in advance. Mark Zuckerberg, the CEO, and founder of Facebook, Inc illustrates this point. Facebook was not the only social media site when it first began. There was MySpace, Friendster and other sites. The reason he excelled is that he wanted it the most, his company was willing to invest the most time, energy, and innovation. Because back then people haven't figured out a way to earn with such sites, they ignored its future potentials. Facebook gave it their all and they dominated the market to become the number one social media site with over 2 billion members.

Take a moment to survey your niche market, what's the competition like? Can you outsmart or outwork them? What is that one thing that if you do will make you stand out immediately from the rest? Identify it and be willing to do what it takes.

Don't Let Technology Fool You, Hard Work Does Pay Off

"Success is never owned, it is rented, and the rent is due every day". Think about this quote by Rory Vaden. Does it make your stomach hurt? That is because the truth is the only cure for the deadly disease called entitlement mindset.

You cannot put in average effort and expect extraordinary results. Technology has made our lives so easy that too many people expect amazing events to just happen, you know because they feel being a human is extraordinary enough.

Everyone wants to give minimum effort and get the maximum results. Like who's going to do the actual work? The four hours work week does not apply when you want to create massive success. Soon, your 8 hours work days can quickly become 10 hours then, 14 hours especially in the beginning phase of your business. Hard work is the key to unlocking freedom, wealth, and peace of mind. The harder you work, the more your luck increases. The system may not be perfect, but you can't deny that we are fortunate to live in a society where anyone can find success if they choose to make the commitment. You can't be entitled and be successful at the same time.

How many people do you know who became billionaires by complaining about what the world owes them? Successful people have realized that their success comes as a result of personal effort and gratitude. While you are looking for all the reasons not to take massive actions, there's someone out there putting in that extra hard work that will give them an edge over you. If you don't work hard, the people who do will get the reward. If no one had to work for what they get, we will all be sitting at home lazy: doing nothing.

You can have whatever you dream of, but you must be willing to put in the extra hours of hard work. If you don't put in the extra hours, then be happy for those who did it because, at the end of the day, the system favors those who add value to it.

SECTION EIGHT:

GET THINGS DONE

CHAPTER 16

Self-discipline

Routines make doing difficult tasks easier, but you need the discipline to force yourself not to rely on motivation. We are so focused on being motivated, only a few people have realized that our brain was not built to withstand tough times for long.

Motivation is only useful for achieving short-term goals. 92% of people who set goals at the beginning of the year can't stick to it. A business is a long-term commitment, you must be able to continue meeting deadlines even when your brain hurts so bad. In the game of success, talent is not enough, and neither is motivation. You must learn to discipline your mind and body to take the right action at the right time. All great business people, philosophers, and leaders describe discipline as the ultimate key to achieving superhuman status.

You cannot manage a successful business without self-discipline. It is a difficult truth to learn but once you master yourself, be assured that you would be surprised how productive you'll become.

How do You Build Self-discipline?

The first step is to make up your mind about what you want to achieve. Do you want to read a book a month, go for a run at 5:00 am or learn to network better even if you suffer from social anxiety?

The next step is to break down the behavior you want to change by asking yourself why you want to achieve that goal in the first place. Ask yourself why you procrastinate. Why do you always feel the need to have a drink before every meeting? When you do this, you awaken your brain to the problem.

And, finally, make a robust plan of how this goal will be achieved.

This final step is the reason many people don't succeed. Planning gives you control of your actions and helps you measure your progress. Most people have never systematically achieved anything because school fails to teach us the process of self-discipline. Students cultivate a habit of waiting until the last minute for supernatural motivation before they prepare for a test or write a report.

Real life, especially in the business world, is far from the reality on campus. People who rely on their feelings when starting a business quickly realize that it no longer feels good to work 10 – 16 hours a day. Soon, they become lazy and fail to see beyond the moment. They give up on the business before it had a chance to take off. Self-discipline is the key to overcoming all of that.

When you master these tasks, you become consistent. Tasks like keeping up with your numbers, agreements, meetings, and marketing become a part of who you are rather than something you have to do. Self-discipline is like a muscle, the more you do it, the easier it becomes. It takes time, concentration, patience, and determination to keep yourself on track: but at the end of the day, you'll discover that learning how to discipline yourself is worth every ounce of sweat you put into it.

Discipline is the unseen magic of what makes successful people who they are. If you can't get yourself to show up every single day, then you are setting yourself up for failure. Successful people do not just get it right one time, they hustle until it becomes a habit. Starting, managing, and growing a business requires you to be accountable.

Mastering self-discipline is all about focusing on finishing one task at a time or setting up a routine. The amazing reality of disciplining yourself is that it has a ripple effect. Once you learn how to read books frequently, you will soon notice your focus improves and your thought process becomes better too. If there's only one thing you learn from this book, let it be that without self-discipline, no matter how positive, passionate or motivated you are, you can't achieve true success.

Unleash Your Positive Energy with Self-discipline

Developing and practicing a positive mindset involves a great deal of self-discipline. Self-discipline is defined as a positive effort in an attempt to develop new habits, thoughts, and actions toward improving yourself and reaching your goals. Practicing self-discipline adds the element of self-control to your life. It provides you with inner strength and ability to stick to the decisions you make. Self-discipline helps you:

- Avoid acting on impulse.

- Overcome procrastination and negativity.

- Fulfill the promises you make.

An easy way to practice self-discipline and work on taking initiative is to schedule a small task for a specific time of the day.

- Schedule a task that will take no longer than 15 minutes to complete during a specific time of the day; preferably in the morning or in the evening.

- When the time of scheduled task rolls around, begin the task. This could be something like writing an email, reading, taking a walk, etc.

- Stick to the schedule for 30 days.

Learning to follow a schedule will help you focus on your priorities and build your confidence in your ability to get things done. Track your progress and keep a record of your accomplishments. This will help reinforce your positive thinking and attitude.

Next, apply this practice of scheduling and completing tasks to your thinking habits.

- Schedule a time of day to practice mindful thinking.

- Take 15 minutes looking for ways to use your strength, improve your weaknesses, pursue opportunities and overcome threats.

- When the 15 minutes are up, encourage yourself with positive "I can" self-talk.

- Stick to this for 30 days and log any changes you notice in your attitude.

Self-discipline is all about cultivating the positive attitude you are teaching yourself to operate in. As with anything else, the only way to get good at operating within a positive mindset is to practice. Don't put too much pressure on yourself to develop this attitude overnight. Though self-discipline takes practice it also takes patience; with a little time, it always works.

CHAPTER 17

Take Massive Action

Action is like the heat from the oven that merges all the ingredients and transforms them into a delicious treat.

Without action, everything you've learned in this book won't be of much use to you. Digest this "one hour spent working is more important than a thousand years spent thinking".

There is merit in developing a mindset of success, in adopting a positive attitude, and in learning to love yourself. These habits can continue to serve you in positive ways even when you've built your empire. As important as that is, the action is undoubtedly a crucial aspect of success. You can set goals and change your mindset until you are blue in the face but if you never take action, nothing, in reality will change.

Put an End to Procrastination

Making excuses or setting specific dates to start like the beginning of the New Year won't get you anywhere. We all live in the now, so begin straight away. Putting things off means you will never even get close to making a start.

Making a start doesn't necessarily mean jumping straight into your internet venture without planning. It means taking the first but significant step to making your desire become a reality.

Small subtle changes are like ripples on the water, once they begin the effects will multiply. Making a start can be something as simple as just putting a basic plan together, this will give you structure and sense of purpose.

Fear is the Problem

Many of us fear taking action. We love making lists, forming plans, and learning new techniques but when it comes to putting it all into motion, we freeze. We procrastinate. We hesitate. We find excuses not to work on our goals anymore.

Or, we do take action, but not on the important stuff. We do more research, we refine our plans, we keep ourselves very busy so it seems like we're taking action but, we're actually just killing time. The most common reason for this fear is the fear of commitment.

We are afraid that once we start moving forward, we will be officially locked into our goal and we are suddenly forced to sink or swim. If we can simply avoid taking action, we can remain safely in the planning stage and not risk anything. We can convince ourselves that we did all we could, but it just didn't work out, there were circumstances beyond our control. So, it will seem like it's not our fault that we're not successful.

There is also another reason why taking action seems so hard: it is called sheer intimidation. You can reduce this fear by setting reasonable goals, but we can also be irrationally fearful about moving forward even if our goals seem manageable.

The most effective way to deal with a fear of taking action is to simply disregard it and take action anyway. Feel fear and do it anyways. That sounds like an impossible challenge if you are feeling paralyzed by fear, but you need to understand the fear of taking action vanishes shortly after you begin moving forward. You suddenly realize that you were worrying over nothing, and you actually begin to enjoy making progress. If you keep with it long enough and frequently enough, exhilaration takes over and you find you can't hold yourself back any longer.

If you absolutely feel terrified about taking action, take some time to look over your plans and come up with one small action steps that you can take immediately. Just one! Then take it. Then pick another small action step and take that one too. Continue accomplishing one step at a time and soon you'll be bold enough to face the big challenges.

Take Deliberate and Productive Actions

When you, finally, decide to overcome procrastination, make sure your action steps are focused. Taking random actions can be a good start sometimes as it can help build your confidence. But, ultimately you'll be going in circles. Instead, take a few minutes to identify the key steps that will make the most difference.

Think about the actions that will attract opportunities, get the attention of your target audience, and create steady progress. Then keep up with this process, gradually increasing the size or magnitude of your steps. If you don't see immediate results, don't give up. Keep at it and in a very short period of time you should be feeling much more confident and eager to keep going.

SECTION NINE:

CONSISTENCY

CHAPTER 18

Keep the Fire Burning

Most of us have no problem feeling motivated when we first set our goals, but that inner fire dies pretty quickly sometimes. It might be due to an intimidating obstacle that appears in our path, or a sense of impatience when we don't see results as quickly as we'd like. How do you regain your motivation when you run out of steam, and can you do anything to keep yourself feeling motivated? Yes, you can!

Remember that motivation is a state of mind, just like discouragement. And like all mindsets, you can choose which one you want to focus on.

Here are some great tips for staying motivated, even if you're not yet seeing the results you want:

Remember Your Dream

If you haven't already, write a detailed description of your ultimate dream. Take your time with this and avoid editing yourself. Visualize a mental vision of your dream and consider how it will change your life for the better. Write down as many details as you can. What type of person will you be? How much money will you have? What will your home look like? What will your relationships be like? How will you feel on a daily basis? Write it all down as if it were your reality today and read it to yourself aloud every single day.

When we are confronted by fear and frustration, it's easy to forget what we're fighting for. It's easy to let the importance of our dream dwindle away and hope that maybe "someday" we'll have the determination to make it happen. Don't let your dream die. Keep it sharp and clear in your own mind. Honor it and vow to keep moving toward it, no matter what it takes.

Remind Yourself of Your "Why"

If you find yourself losing steam and feeling overwhelmed by obstacles, take a sheet of paper and write down the benefits of your dream. Remind yourself why you are chasing these goals in the first place.

What will you gain after your internet business goes viral? You may become:

- Famous

- Financially free

- Meet amazing people

- A memorable brand

- A better friend, partner, or parent

- Gain capital to start another business

- A mentor or coach

Write your list of benefit on a sticky note and put where you can read it daily. By doing this, you should be more determined than ever to keep working toward your goals because acceptance of anything less is unthinkable.

See Obstacles as Opportunities for Growth

One of the most common reasons we lose our motivation is because we feel overwhelmed or intimidated by unexpected blocks along the way. You can have the strongest discipline skills in the world, but, without an ability to cope with bumps along the way: you may just give it all up. Rather than allowing this to happen to you, simply choose not to let it bother you.

Say to yourself, "An obstacle is nothing more than a detour on my path. I'll find a way around it because I'm not giving up" thinking about these thoughts will empower you to continue moving forward again, even if you were intimidated initially. Obstacles are as big as you choose to make them. If you groan and loss track, the obstacle will grow bigger and more intimidating. But, if you, instead, shrug your shoulders, roll up your sleeves and face it heads on, the obstacle shrinks to the size of an anthill.

Affirm the Possibilities

Doubt is another motivation killer that stops us from going after our dreams.

When you set your goals, it's exciting, and you are convinced you can do it. But, if the results you're expecting don't show up right away, you start doubting yourself, or doubt if the goal is "realistic" enough. You begin to think that after all: if it was meant to be and/or if you were meant to be successful, it would come naturally to you, right?

Spoiler alert: success is not a hidden superpower that you can just discover inside of you. Even those born into wealth, still need to learn how to maintain their status, or else the money blows away.

If you feel your commitment begin to dwindle, blast the doubt right out of your head by reading success stories of others who have accomplished the impossible. Seek out YouTube videos or television programs about people who have overcome immense personal challenges to achieve success, and affirm that if they did it, you too can do it.

Manage Stress Properly

Sometimes we get so motivated that we might take on too much, too fast and end up feeling burned out. You'll know when this happens to you because you start feeling stressed, overwhelmed, and irritated by even the slightest disruption in your plans.

You start feeling annoyed about having to work on your goals, and decide you'd rather take a nap. Give in to that feeling. Yes, go with it. Climb into bed and have a good rest. Go see a funny movie with a friend, or curl up with a good book by yourself. Go dancing, or sign up for some pottery or painting classes. Do something completely unrelated to your goals, and feel good about it. We all need rest, recreation, and a reminder that there is more to life than chasing our goals.

Enjoying the Journey

Success is a journey, not a destination. It's about what you do and you become along the way.

Success is a process of letting go of perceived limitations, growing and developing as unique individuals: believing in your true potential, honoring the best parts of ourselves and sharing them with the world.

Most of this process takes place in your mind as you've always had the potential to be successful through positive thinking and hard work. You only need to believe and embrace it.

You Can Never Go Wrong with An Attitude Of Gratitude

Gratitude can transform any aspect of your life especially your thoughts. When you feel grateful for the good things in your life, you are obviously focusing more on them. This not only helps you to feel more positive on a regular basis, it also helps you to worry less about the negative events, lack, and struggle.

You feel happier and everything in your life tends to run more smoothly. You feel optimistic, blessed, and grateful for the opportunity to mold your life into a work of art. Beginning today, make it a habit to express a feeling of gratitude for all the wonderful things you have.

At first you may struggle to find things to be grateful for especially when your business doesn't seem to be getting much attention. Start with the most obvious: at least you have the opportunity, resources, zeal, health, and time to pursue your goals. So many people have given up on themselves years ago, but you, you've stayed focused.

- Say this to yourself:

"I'm grateful for my healthy body, my ability to see and hear, the love of my family and friends."

Keep practicing, soon you'll noticing more things to feel grateful for.

SECTION TEN:

YOU DESERVE HAPPINESS

CHAPTER 19

What Makes You Happy

Happiness is a choice: you either decide to look on the bright side or see the glass half empty.

When we think of being successful, you may imagine that happiness is an inevitable side effect. We may envision ourselves with the perfect house, the perfect partner, the perfect children, and millions of dollars in your account. And you believe that all of that stuff will make you happy.

Sorry to burst your bubble, that's a skewed view of reality. Material things and other people cannot make you happy, only you can make yourself happy. And it all begins with a choice.

Do you believe that? If you are experiencing challenges or lack, your mind will probably sarcastically reply "Yeah right, it's that easy". But think about this: why are there so many rich and unhappy people in the world? Simple, it's because money and success do not automatically create happiness. Neither does power, status, romance, or your possessions. We simply believe they do because we are looking outside of ourselves for the solution to our problems.

The more money you have, the bigger your problems will be. You may get sued, lose sleep, and most of the people you meet may only like you because you are rich. It's going to be easy to handle these issues if you learn to be happy now.

How Do You Learn to be Happy?

Happiness is a personal concept that is different for each of us. Take a moment to consider what happiness means to you. That's one important step in understanding how you can bring more happiness into your life.

Think about the people, places, and things that fill you with joy and peace. Do you feel happiest when you're at home, or at work? How about when you're spending time with friends and loved ones? Or when you're reading an uplifting book, watching a funny movie, or donating your time to help others? Whatever activities you enjoy the most, make an effort to bring more of them into your life.

It's easy for us to sabotage ourselves by placing restrictions on our happiness. We affirm that we'll be happy if this or that happens but, completely ignore other possibilities. Of course, certain situations just aren't pleasant no matter what – but for the most part, we can choose to enjoy most of our experiences and outcomes: even if they aren't what we originally expected.

Most importantly your willingness to accept that happiness is mostly a result of the choices you make: you'll put in the effort to ensure every moment is worth it regardless of your surroundings.

Happiness is not a gift you deserve: it's already within you. All you need to do is choose to embrace it. This can be easier said than done: but, with consistent practice, you'll get there. Learning how to be happy on a basic level is one of the most important skills you could ever have. Perfection is a delusion: acknowledge that your life will never be just right, give yourself permission to enjoy the moments.

SECTION ELEVEN:

JUST BEFORE YOU BEGIN

CHAPTER 20

Start Your Business Right

"Have the courage to face the truth. Do the right thing because it is right. These are the magic keys to living your life with integrity" - **W. Clement Stone**

Too many people think starting an online business will immediately give them the personal and financial freedom they've always dreamed of. That is very far from the truth.

Having your own business is tough. You are your own employer and employee. Interpreneurship has become the cool pop culture thing of the 21st century. CEOs like Jeff Bezos, Elon Musk, and Mark Zuckerberg glamorized lifestyle lure unsuspecting naive people who expect to push a button to be the next big thing.

Remeber this, 8 out of every 10 businesses fail in their first two years. Interpreneurship is not for everyone: if you decide it is your path to a fulfilled life, then prepare your mind for the grind. There are no vacations when starting a business, and you must commit fully to making your dreams a reality. It's a lonely journey at the beginning, you'll need to put in a ton of effort to get that idea off the ground.

You may not necessarily require knowledge of the legal and structural aspect of the business at the beginning, but self-mastery and the cash flow are necessary prerequisites for every successful business. Your journey will be made easier if you begin with a simpler version of your idea.

Amazon.com began as a book retail website: today, it's the biggest online retail business ever built. Ideas are amazing: your idea may sound very promising to you, but it must be profitable for it to become an actual business.

Everyone has ideas, what determines who succeed and those that fail miserably is the manner of execution. When starting out, your attention should be focused on the most important things first.

The foundation of every business is sales. In the case of an internet business, its conversions and ad revenue. Through this, more money becomes available which accelerates your growth. Your priority right now is to focus on what brings in the cash.

It is crucial that you plan the execution of your online startup around making as many conversions as possible. I know Mark Zuckerberg and other tech companies built their businesses without initial cashflow plans, I am not referring to them. Unless you are creating a Silicon Valley unicorn, you need money, and you need it fast.

Before deciding to start your business, the plan must not be perfect, still, you need to plan. That is how great corporations come to be, life has no direct standard rules for achieving greatness.

Some people might get lucky enough to know the end game of their business while others have to keep planning, implementing and evaluating as they grow. You are the biggest asset of your business: your passion, drive, energy is what will fuel the business especially in the first few years. That is why it is very essential for you to master your mindset.

Success is never an accident, it is always a result of intentional effort. Refused to be at the mercy of the market and start right. The problem with young people these days is that they focus their attention too much on worshiping those who have succeeded, instead, of creating their own reality.

Everyone wants fast everything now: fast food, fast cars, fast money, fast love. Technology has made our lives so much easier and it's true, you can achieve fast success if you choose to work for it. It is now easier to network, connect with people, share your ideas with the world, and reach your customers.

Then why are so many people still struggling to find success? The answer is obvious. Technology has made our lives so easy that our minds have become too weak to understand the value of effort and patience. Read that statement again if you need to.

We are living in the most amazing and opportunity-filled time in history, yet productivity globally is dropping to record low. The productivity rate of the US is declining each year, not surprising the United Kingdom is having similar problems.

Have you noticed the same problem in your life? You spend so much time doing stuff but never actually achieving the things you truly need to. It's not just a national and personal issue, it is a major problem for startups too. Overexcited internet entrepreneurs think they have the most innovative idea of all time, they venture into business without a good realistic plan and a few months later, they've failed. The worst part is that most of these businesses that fails never quite understand the reason for their failure.

Do you want your online business to succeed? Then focus on the productive aspect of actively turning visitors, followers, or fans into conversions.

Your online startup will succeed as long as you have products or service that people are willing to pay for, and a realistic plan to execute it. It's fascinating how entrepreneurs still get this wrong.

All ideas are great until you ask people to pay for it. When you understand this basic principle of building profitability, your business becomes less of a struggle. Don't rush into it, there will always be ideas, and a market ready to buy. Competition is good, but it should not be the only thing pushing your business growth. Companies like Nokia who left the rubber production industry to make cell phones failed when they could no longer offer valuable smartphones to consumers. You need to understand yourself, your product and the audience that will pay for it.

Top Skills You Need When Starting an Online Business

Successful interpreneurs are people who have mastered the right skills sets that are required to survive in this super competitive hustle. They are not the smartest, the most hardworking or the most privileged people on the planet.

Although hard work is crucial to being successful, it's not the only skill you need. Remember, if you don't learn and do what is required of you, failure is pretty much guaranteed. It's uncertain that you will succeed if you have all the skills, but it will significantly increase your chances of making your dreams come true.

In business, the more you learn and work, the more your luck increases. There are no shortcuts, how many successful entrepreneurs do you know that work four hours a week beside Tim Ferris? None.

Success is a continuous journey of effort and reward, if you stop growing, you will eventually stop making money. There are over seven billion people on planet earth. What type of secret idea do you think you have that others cannot compete against? The nerve of every business is a growth mindset, and for you to succeed at constantly tackling the challenges there are some key skills you need to have in other to get it right.

Below is a list of the most important skills online entrepreneurs must have.

- You must,

    - evolve by analyzing and adapting to how the internet changes.

    - Develop a positive and successful mindset.

    - Be productive.

    - Invest your time wisely.

    - Learn internet marketing especially through social media.

    - Learn the art of branding.

    - Understand copywriting (even if you intend to hire a copywriter to do it for you).

    - Think Creatively.

- Learn about customer engagement.

- Tell amazing stories.

- Think critically.

- Connect with (people through your passion and enthusiasm).

- Be original.

- Negotiate.

- Plan.

- Be patient.

- Understand trends.

- Work independently.

Your business chances of survival depend on you, develop the right skills and improve your odds of making your vision a reality.

CHAPTER 21

Failure Does Not Define You

"Failure is the opportunity to begin again, more intelligently"- **Henry Ford**

The biggest reason why most people never get started is because they are afraid of failure. The fear of the unknown is common in our society. Age does not matter when it comes to how we deal with failure; society has conditioned our minds that failure is bad and should be avoided at all cost. That is why so many people rather stay passive than risk failing.

The voice in our head reminds us every time we want to try something new of all the possible "what ifs". The problem is not what if you fail, but how will you handle it. Always remember that, failure is only a stepping stone to success. There are zero people on the planet who have succeeded without overcoming failure.

Failure prepares you for success. You may not like to hear that but it's the truth. If you do not fail, you may never learn how to get ahead. The thought of Failing should not stop you from going after your goals.

Imagine if Thomas Edison stopped trying just because he failed or if the Wright brothers gave up after their first crash. Our world will be a completely different place today without the persistence of great men. Failure is never what we want but it's unavoidable on your way to success.

- Steve Jobs once said that, "Sometimes life hits you in the head with a brick. Don't lose faith".

Do everything you can to succeed and if things don't turn out as expected, take it as an opportunity to grow. Picking yourself up after failing is the true definition of courage. There are no failures, only prospects to learn.

The only time you fail is when you quit. People may tell you to give up, it may seem like it's impossible to achieve and you're running out of resources, but never let life keep you down. Keep your mind on the opportunities and not the problem. Winston Churchill saved an entire nation and the world by encouraging people not to give up. If not for

Churchill's persistence, the British would have given in to Hitler's rule.

There will be days when it looks like your effort is not being rewarded: focusing your mind on how far you've come keeps you persistent. Living a purposeful life requires you to be brave enough to confront the challenges you face. The fear of failure should not deny you the life you've always dreamed of. Always remind yourself of your purpose daily, and that no matter what, never give up.

CONCLUSION

You have made the right choice to become an internet entrepreneur. Interpreneurship may be hard at first but, with a positive mindset, optimistic attitude, hard work, and dedication: you'd be surprised how easy it is to succeed.

"The whole culture is telling you to hurry, while the art tells you to take your time. Always listen to the art" - **Junot Díaz**

The biggest challenge we all face in achieving our goals is getting started. Pushing through the fear and taking initiative is half the battle. Life has its twist and turns, but we have always thrived. You cannot afford wishful thinking, get your ideas out there. You can dominate your niche if you have the right mindset.

Despite the fear-mongering, millions of people just like you are making a killing from their online business. They took the bold initiative to sell what they believe in. You don't need to have the best product or offer the best service: you just need to own your brand identity: soon the fans and followers will come.

Now that you understand the why principle: use it to tell great stories and connect on a deep level with your audience. Clear your mind of distracting thoughts and keep your focus on the one thing that makes your brand stand out. It's not okay to just want success, you must commit to mastery. You must act now and be loyal to your goals.

There's a French proverb which says the future is purchased by today. It's not about that one magical moment, but the little things you do every day. Always keep your mind focused on the goal, while enjoying the moment. Embrace positivity - you'll need it to overcome. Crush the negativity every time it raises its ugly head. Only you can determine how far you are willing to go.

Remember your journey to success can be as easy or as difficult as you make it. Practice using affirmations if you find yourself struggling with negative thoughts. Change your vocabulary, use positive assertive words that confirm your excellence. Tell yourself that no one got you like you do. Surround yourself with like-minded people who inspire you.

In every step of the way, trust yourself, trust the journey, trust that the universe got you. You can carve a niche for yourself like many other successful entrepreneurs have done.

You are supported: the universe supports you, people will support you: your ideas, goals, visions, plans, and strategy for success are all supported. You rule your destiny, you rule your mind. Decide today that you won't be defeated by the bumps on the way.

You can achieve any height in life if you improve the quality of your thoughts, question your beliefs, take bold actions and evolve. Open your mind to the possibilities: life is not a bed of roses but, if you choose to be proactive, your online venture will grab the attention of hungry buyers all over the globe. It's okay to make mistakes as long as you learn from them. Avoid the blame game, it only hurts your growth.

Trust in your ideas, decisions, and originality: believe that what you have to offer is valuable and embrace the abundance. Just as your negative mindset have limited you in the past, your positive mindset will get you pumped up for success. Visualize it, go ahead and convince yourself that all you've ever wanted is at your fingertips. You can achieve anything you want once you decide to work hard for it. Relax! Have fun: you're in this for the long run.

THANK YOU, INTERPRENEURS!

Thank you for taking the time to read this book. You are on your road to becoming a successful internet entrepreneur! Every book is like a child to its writer. So, when someone enjoys it, it becomes a delightful moment for the writer. I hope this book will guide you towards the right path, and I encourage you to take the right step.

You should nurture your dream of being an internet entrepreneur. It's never too late pursuing your dreams! I recommend you to apply whatever you have learned from this book immediately. Being an entrepreneur is not an easy task and the use of the internet in your business is the next level skill. Yes, it is the next level skill because it's changing rapidly. What is an awesome idea right now can be a dead-end tomorrow. So, act fast and act wisely.

You have to make up your mind first. I have already told you that the road to success is never easy but with the right mindset and attitude, you can accomplish anything! All successful internet entrepreneurs have faced these same problems you are facing now. What they have learned from their mistakes is priceless, and you can find all these tips in this book. I have also shared opportunities and new trends online. If this book encourages you, then I will consider myself successful.

Below you will find a link to my website where I regularly discuss internet marketing trends and opportunities. Don't forget to subscribe for the regular newsletter and stay up to date.

Feel free to contact me for any questions or suggestions regarding this book at my website, twitter or facebook page. I always like hearing from my readers, and I would enjoy hearing from you!

If any part of this book helps you to the journey of INTERPRENEURSHIP, then don't forget to share the idea with others and recommend them to collect this book. Also, I humbly request you to give a feedback which will encourage me to write again. A positive feedback not only encourages its author but also encourages others to read it. Should great ideas not be contained right?

Thank you again for reading this far. Enlighten yourself. Don't forget to use the idea which has just sparkled into your mind. CEO of Alibaba, Jack Ma, once said,

"Before 30 years old, it's not which company you go to, it's which boss you follow that's very important. A good boss teaches you differently. At the age of 30-40, you need to think very clearly. If you really want to be an entrepreneur, you need to start working for yourself."

I wish you all the best towards your success.

Jeralyn Pasinabo Peagler

www.jp360solutions.com

Follow @jp360solutions on Facebook, Instagram, Twitter or LinkedIn

INDEX

187

www.ingramcontent.com/pod-product-compliance
Lightning Source LLC
Chambersburg PA
CBHW060555200326
41521CB00007B/575